the MASTER ATTRACTOR

Also by
Dr. Mandy (Menahem) Lender

The Vision of Habakkuk.
The Law of Attraction in the Holy Bible

the MASTER
ATTRACTOR

The Law of Attraction in the Holy Bible & Beyond

MANDY (MENAHEM) LENDER, MD

NEW YORK

the MASTER ATTRACTOR
The Law of Attraction in the Holy Bible & Beyond

TABLE OF CONTENTS

Let there be light; and there was light (Genesis 1:3)

CHAOS IN ORION
A Hubble telescope photograph. Courtesy of NASA

Thou shalt also decree a thing and it shall be
Established unto thee:
And the light shall shine upon thy ways.
Job 22:28

PART ONE

THE LAW OF ATTRACTION

INTRODUCTION

The Law of Attraction is a mindset. With this mindset you can literally watch how your thoughts turn into reality. In order to align yourself with the mindset of the Law of Attraction (LOA) you need to assimilate its framework and its Key Concepts. The LOA is universal. It prevails over our lives whether we are aware of it or not. The LOA is pervasive and is not subject to our consent. It just is.

Veronica is the dental hygienist who helps me keep my teeth in good shape. She helps me attract health (and wealth). Veronica asked me while I was seated on her dental chair, "What is your book all about?"

I paused for a moment, mostly because I could not close my mouth to speak. Then I answered, "My book is about the intersection of neuro-science, social psychology, and old-time Biblical wisdom."

Note I did not simply say that my book is about the Law of Attraction. Actually, I should have said the book is about *"turning your thoughts into reality."* No matter what my answer would be, I received the same response: "Huh."

Or it may have been, *"Huh?"*

I find it difficult to explain to folks of all walks of life that they are in control of their life; that they attract their circumstances and create their own reality. Most people do not want to take responsibility for their own life. Some of my patients do not want to take responsibility for their own health. "It's in my genes," they like to argue. "It's the Holidays, you know. It's Thanksgiving— you can't stop eating."

They would rather leave it to government to decide, or to their parents, or do what they do to please their psychotherapist. Or please their Rabbi or spouse.

It is difficult for folks to accept the premise that we are responsible for attracting our circumstances, and we co-create our reality.

Didn't you attract your spouse? Or did the priest or rabbi attract your bride to you?

Yes, I know in certain parts of the globe parents still arrange a suitable marriage partner for their children...

The point of this book is that we are co-creators of our life circumstances and the great news is that we can, by and large, control those circumstances and our immediate reality.

∽⟨⟩⟨⟩∾

In the last one hundred and fifty years, a movement consisting of thinkers, teachers and authors emerged, to describe a phenomenon called the Law of Attraction (LOA). A book titled *Thoughts Are Things* was published in 1889.[1]

On the same vein, Walter Wintle[2] published a poem titled *Think*, circa the same period.

The author, Robert Collier, published a more extensive work titled *The Secret of the Ages*.[3] He outlined seven "secrets" of the LOA. He also used the term *Law of Abundance*.[4]

Modern authors who dealt with the Law of Attraction described it as a rediscovered development in human thought and behavior. Today there

---

1   Prentice Mulford (1834–1891). Re-published by Wilder Publications. Radford VA. 2008.
2   Walter D. Wintle was a poet who lived in the late 19th and early 20th century. Little is known about his life. He is best known for writing the world famous poem "*Thinking*," also known as "*The Man Who Thinks He Can.*"
3   Robert collier: "The Secret of the Ages." Robert Collier Book Corporation. Ramsey NJ. 27th edition 1975.
4   Robert Collier, 1885–1950. Nephew of the founder of Collier's Weekly. His best quote is: "*The first principle of success is desire--knowing what you want.*"

are countless legends in the formats of reports, books, and documentary movies, written, produced and published; as well as live classes and webinars, explaining the LOA phenomenon. The LOA in practice advises people to choose their thoughts carefully because built-in dynamic forces of thought in the human mind stir, drive and compel the thinking person towards manifesting their thoughts into reality. Some authors described the LOA as a modern development, as if they were surprised by its existence. Still others referred to it as a secret waiting to be revealed by them to the world. Post-modern authors try to leave the impression that the LOA is somehow a recent discovery, or an innovation impressively associated with the science called "quantum physics." The LOA preceded the field of quantum physics by millennia.

The Holy Bible tells stories with life lessons drawn from these tales. If you accept the notion that the Bible is a repository of the collective wisdom of the ages, then the Law of Attraction is available to the reader of the Bible.

The Bible—consists of the Hebrew Bible (the Old Testament) and the New Testament. The Old Testament is a Christian term denoting the Hebrew Bible that is the holy scripture of the Jewish faith. It is an inspired anthology of writings by many authors over two millennia. The first writings began probably two thousand and eight hundred years ago. During the last twenty-three centuries, individuals, scribes, translators, scholars, theologians and committees of editors did their inspired best to right-write, edit, translate and re-translate the Holy Scriptures, as we know them today. For me the Bible is a great repository of the best of the collective human experience and wisdom.

Now think about it—if the LOA is as powerful and as compelling as its various proponents and teachers claim it to be, then it had to be present in the stories and life-lessons canonized in the Bible. Indeed, we find a wealth of evidence for the presence of the Law of Attraction in the Bible.

"New age" and "new thought" terms such as "energy" or "vibrations" are not mentioned in the Bible.

However, the actual mindset and effects of the LOA on human endeavors are vividly described there. If anything, it is the information age that drew attention to and publicized the Law of Attraction that was laying there before the Bible was written and canonized.

Consider that:
For the Law of Attraction to be described in the Bible—Its existence must have preceded the authors and editors of the Bible.

Readers and students of the Law of Attraction who want to understand the LOA and who want to witness how the LOA is also grounded in the biblical writings will find ample evidence in this book, illustrating the universal nature of the LOA in the human experience.

Chapter One

WHAT IS THE LAW OF ATTRACTION

A s thinkers, we are co-creators of our reality.

The aphorism, *thoughts become things,* has its early origins in one form or another in the Holy Bible. Both the Hebrew Bible and the New Testament tell this same pearl of wisdom by the ancient sages in various nuances. *As a man thinketh so is he.* (Proverbs 23:7).

KEY CONCEPT:

Thinking people co-create their reality.

How Does The Law Of Attraction Operate

Let us explain in modern terms how we account for the phenomenon of the LOA.

The essence of the process is that *a thought once sparked in a human mind, starts thinking about itself.* In due course, that thought spawns collateral thoughts.[5] We often call them *associated thoughts,* known commonly as "associations." Next, the new collateral associated thoughts spread throughout the mind as a ripple around the original thought. The ripples of thoughts expand our consciousness to include the target idea that we wish to manifest in our reality.

The human brain has within its anatomical structures a framework of inter-connected neuronal circuits that is called the *Reticular Activating System.* This neuronal network is believed to mediate shifts from relaxed awareness (sleepiness) to intensified attentive interest. Blood flow is increased in the areas of the midbrain reticular formation during performance of mental tasks requiring increased alertness. The increase in blood flow is believed to be a marker of increased neuronal activity. The increased blood flow is an indication of heightened cognitive alertness and awareness.

In addition, neuroscientists described in recent years another neuronal system in the brain that is called the brain's *"default mode network."* This "default mode network" is always active, even at sleep, busily processing memories and information, or daydreaming. It is thought that this neuronal default network is coordinating other parts of the brain and preparing it to get its tasks accomplished in alignment with the person's conscious thoughts of objectives and intentions.

As our consciousness expands, we start to see new possibilities—we conceive of questions to ask and actions to take. We make synchronized associations with various concurrent events that occur around us. We start to receive invitations to participate in related events, or even to receive our desired wish or object.

Often—a better outcome may be delivered to us.

---

5   Certain post-modern teachers of the LOA use the words *vibration* synonymously with the term *thought.*

THE LOA AS AN INTERNET SEARCH ENGINE

Compare this mind process described above to your use of an internet search engine: Google, Yahoo or Bing. You are interested in an item and you enter the name of the item into the search engine and press Enter. Then, *voila*, the search engine returns to you thousands or millions of related information items in a split moment, or while you still type the item. It does not matter to the search engine what you entered—an object or a thought. Both are *things* for the search engine. Or, if you insist, both are energy signals to the search engine.

The search engine does not care and does not pass any judgment on the item you asked for information. Better yet, the search engine does not care if what you search is "true" or "false."

You always get what you ask for from the search engine. You get it in the form of links leading you to your desired objective. With the links to information you can now get to assemble and manifest your objective. You literally get a map to your destination with *turn by turn directions* to your destination, if that is a place you asked for.

Thus, we become co-creators of our new reality and this new reality starts to manifest and take shape around us.

As described above, now that we think about "it" (whatever "it" may be), we start to see and perceive evidence for it all around us. When we perceive the conscious evidence for "it," we start to believe that "it" is truly our empiric reality.

Thus, repeated thinking and vivid imagination of a desired (or undesired) situation is eventually and inevitably manifested in the surrounding reality of the thinker.

The term LOA is a misnomer. It is neither a "law" nor a decree. It is a consistent obligatory series of physiological, psychological and behavioral processes, ingrained in every human-being's nervous system.

The Law of Attraction is *a neurophysiologic phenomenon that matches our target seeking thoughts with the corresponding components of reality—the reality that is in alignment with our original thought.*

Here is a profound point for the reader to keep in mind.

If the thinker holds contradictory doubts about the desired outcome (the "new reality"), the central nervous system enters a state of confusion and will not deliver the desired outcome. Or, if the thinker believes that he or she does not deserve whatever "it" is they desire—they block the manifestation of the desire into their life.

I find it amusing to read reports in the media that the "LOA doesn't work" or "the LOA is a scam." The LOA "does not work" when the thinker is confused or doubts its existence.

In other words: *as you believe so it is done unto you.* (Mark 11:24).

In order to benefit from the LOA you have to think and live in alignment with the Law of Attraction.

⤧⟡⤸

THE PSYCHOLOGY OF THE LAW OF ATTRACTION

In the previous sections we presented facts drawn from the field of neuro-anatomy and neuro-physiology. We compared the brain-mind operations to an internet search engine that collects relevant data from various storage devices on servers around the world. The relevance of each piece of data is considered and weighed in relation to the original question or item request. Each item brought up by the search engine may or may not advance the researcher towards their goal or objective. The search engine is just an extension of the human brain for this purpose. Thirty years ago data search and collection was done manually in libraries in front of index card-size catalogue drawers. Those physical catalogues are gone and replaced by computerized data bases. The computerized data bases are aggregated to bring the information to you through the global search engines. Your mind still searches for information to zero-in on its target. These days your mind acquires the data through highly efficient means from wider sources but the *final judgment of the relevance of the data is done by your mind.*

The relevant points of data that you acquire are the matching components that the LOA aggregated for you in order to manifest that which you desire.

This is great news—the LOA is now made easier and works faster.

❧❦

The Self-Fulfilling Prophecy And Social Psychology

In this section we review what researchers and thinkers know about the Law of Attraction in the sciences of sociology and psychology.

A *self-fulfilling prophecy* is both an extension and a variant of the LOA.

Modern social studies define self-fulfilling prophecy as a prediction that directly or indirectly causes it to become true by the very terms of the prophecy itself due to feedback between the believer, the subsequent behavior and the resulting outcome.

During the years 1923–1928 the sociologist, Walter Isaac Thomas, stated in his writings:

If men define situations as real, they are real in their consequences.

This statement is known as the *Thomas theorem.*

In his writing, Thomas stated further that any definition of a situation will influence the present. The individual that is involved in pronouncing a definition of a situation makes gradual personality and lifestyle changes to maintain their personal congruency with the situation.

This last paragraph is just the same statement that marketing experts and advertisers knew: *perception is reality.*

❧❦

The influential social scientist, Robert K. Merton (1910–2003), defined the term "*self-fulfilling prophecy,*" its structure and its consequences.[6] Self-fulfilling prophecy may at the beginning be an arbitrary or false definition of a situation. By eliciting new behavior it transforms the newly defined situation into a reality. The original "prophet" will cite the course of events as proof that he was right from the beginning.

A "prophecy" that is declared as "truth," even if it is an arbitrary "truth," may influence people through fear or through logical confusion to behave in a manner that fulfills the "prophecy."

---

6   Robert K. Merton: Social Theory and Social Structure. 1968. New York Free Press.

The sequence of events that causes the change in peoples' behavior is very likely a result of mental *cognitive dissonance*. The *cognitive dissonance* is a mental discomfort consisting of anxiety or guilt and results from holding two conflicting opinions or beliefs at the same time. The way to reduce the level of the dissonance or get rid of it is by changing attitudes and beliefs. Getting in alignment with new beliefs is one way to eliminate the cognitive dissonance. Sometimes people use blaming of others, or denial of reality, to avoid the disagreeable feeling of cognitive dissonance.

In clinical practice it is well known that requiring a diabetic patient to perform home blood sugar testing using a glucometer and maintaining a written log of the observed blood sugar levels is sufficient to effect a small but measurable reduction in the blood sugar levels without additional anti-diabetic medications.

Another clinical example is the *placebo* effect of a presumed medication or sham procedure that relieves pain but in reality is an inert pill or capsule or sham surgery.

The contrary phenomenon is a *nocebo* effect caused by a sham procedure or inert medication where a patient was warned about potential side-effects that may aggravate the patient's pain or discomfort. After the treatment the patient complains of new pain or side-effects of the treatment.

In the internet age, patients have easy access to pharmacologic information including possible and rare side-effects. The patient experiences a discomfort or fear and may discontinue the prescribed ethical and beneficial therapy because of the warning they read about side-effects, included in the medication's patient education insert.

When individuals know they are being observed—even not in response to an experimental manipulation—their behavior changes. This change in behavior is known as the *Hawthorne effect*. It is a form of behavior modification by people who improve or modify an aspect of their practice when they are aware that their practice is measured or observed.

Since automated pharmacy management technology was introduced it became possible to measure drug utilization by prescribing medical practitioners. Some physicians tend to favor certain medications more than others. When presented with drug utilization data of their practice compared to their peers, most practitioners change their practice pattern without any further suggestion. They do it because of the cognitive discomfort caused to them when realizing that they are different than the majority of their peers.

The point that we make is that the perceptions of the individual change through factual or suggestive influences. When the perception of reality changes—a change in behavior, or practice and activity—ensues.

THREE PREDICATES OF THE LAW OF ATTRACTION

Three predicates to remember about the Law of Attraction.

First—the LOA is involuntary and incessantly creating.

It happens all the time in the human mind. We humans always think; one way or another, good or bad, consciously or unconsciously, while we are awake or during our sleep. We make ceaseless mental selections for good or for bad that manifest in our lives.

Second—the LOA creates and manifests in our reality with minimal time delays.

If there seems to be a time gap from mental conception to empiric manifestation, it is caused by our mental doubts and disbeliefs. Quoting William Shakespeare: *"Our doubts are traitors that make lose the good we are fearing to attempt."* Take note that the concept of delay is a relative time-concept. It is a matter of human perception of time. A delay of 100 years is a tiny blip in the chronology of our green and blue planet Earth, or in the chronology of the universe.

Third—the process of creation and manifestation is effortless.

Indeed in theory it is effortless. If manifestation comes about with difficulties and efforts it is because we hold antagonistic thoughts and doubts towards the goal, the intent or the outcome. The doubts and mixed feelings exert the slowing brakes on the process of attraction of the components that are required for manifestation.

KEY CONCEPTS OF THE LAW OF ATTRACTION

The LOA has a framework.

The framework consists of ten Key Concepts or underlying principles of habit. We shall review the Key Concepts throughout this and the following chapters. The Key Concepts will be mentioned whenever relevant throughout this book. The Key Concepts will be repeated in the form of examples throughout the book. They are also listed as a summary at the end of the book.

Alongside these Key Concepts, we shall review certain *tools* that people use to trigger or activate the LOA into action and manifest desired reality or outcome. The tools are either certain habits of thinking or behavioral practices in alignment with the LOA that bring predictable results. The behavioral practices are skill sets.

Throughout the review of the biblical masters' stories, teachings and leadership actions, we see that these grand masters of the LOA in the Bible conformed knowingly or unknowingly with the Key Concepts of the LOA in content of thought or their personal conduct. The biblical masters used the tools that trigger the LOA in their activities and the contents of their ethos conformed to the framework and Key Concepts of the LOA.

⋯⋯

COMMON TOOLS THAT TRIGGER THE LOA

Various "tools" are suggested on how to practice manifesting thoughts into reality.

An example of a common tool is practicing the thought-sequence of Ask, Believe, Receive. In that case the thinker-petitioner *asks* for a desired condition, or declares an intention to achieve an objective. The petitioner maintains a state of *belief* that the objective is being fulfilled through his or her readiness to *receive* the manifested outcome or a better one.

Other common simple tools of related nature include:

- A repeated *prayer* for a desired condition.
- *Writing* down a desired outcome as a goal.
- Emotionally imagining and *visualizing* a desired outcome in the mind's eye associated with arousing excitement.
- Giving *thanks* for the desired outcome, before it is manifested.

Certain contemporary authors suggest that declaring an intention with sincere willingness to act, and taking some *action* is sufficient to bring about the desired outcome.

We shall also see how writing a goal or intent is a potent tool. And better yet, a *written prayer request* combines the last two tools into a synergistic powerful manifesting practice.

⟿⟾

All these methods work. A combination of these methods is synergistically more effective to bring about the desired manifestation.

In the next chapters, we shall review biblical reports of actual manifestations. Many of these manifestations were considered "miracles." We shall comment on these manifestations to indicate which tool or "mechanism" the biblical figure seems to have employed or practiced.

The Bible is replete with stories that illustrate the LOA. Creation and co-creation begins in Genesis, chapter 1. Although the story of the creation seems straight forward, it provides a valuable lesson that has not diminished in its significance in human history to the present day.[7]

⟿⟾

A Tool: Declaring An Intent Or Objective

The first occurrence, in which an idea was pronounced in a declarative format and was instantly manifested, is found right at the beginning—in Genesis 1:3.[8] A divine idea was expressed—*let there be light*. And, there was light. The course of creation continued for six days through manifesting divine ideas into empiric reality. Genesis 1:26–27, describes this process for the creation of humans. I just indicate that an idea and its declared utterance can manifest into a reality that is perceived empirically by human beings' senses. Note that after this first manifestation by declaration, subsequent declarations of intent by the Divine were followed by an action verb. In the case of creating "a man,"

---

7   I wish to make it clear that I do not make here a personal statement in favor of one theory or another, i.e., creationism or evolution. I treat it here as it is—a story.

8   All Bible quotes are KJV.

the biblical text reads: "*Let us **make** a man.*"⁹ The verb *to make* indicates that a certain action was taken.

The lesson we learned here is that creation often require some form of *doing* or acting to be exercised by the creator or co-creator. In a subsequent chapter, we shall see an example of "inspired action."

⋙⋘

Another example is found in the gospels. Matthew 7:7, Luke 11:9; and Mark 11:24, tell us that Jesus the Teacher preached a similar concept: *Ask and it shall be given you.*

The gospels have no specific advice on what to ask, or instructions on how to ask. There are no limitations on how much to ask.

The format is Ask, Believe, and it is Given.

It may be assumed that the asking is also done in the form of prayer. Prayer for that purpose is not the required tool by the gospels in this context. However it is a powerful tool that works.

⋙⋘

You may now think that I make it sound simplistic and easy when I say that all we have to do is declare intent. Well, it can be easy. Here is what Eliphaz the Temanite¹⁰ told Job: "*Thou shall also decree a thing and it shall be established unto thee and the light shall shine upon thy ways.*" (Job 22:28).

Let us take a methodic break to parse this verse and appreciate its profound implications. All a person needs to do is to know what to think about—the intent or condition you want. Then you *shall decree a thing.*

Declare your intent!

If you do that—*light shall shine upon thy ways.* That means you will see your ways (your path to progress) to accomplish your decree (objective). The path for manifestation should be effortless. Be sure to keep your objective short and simple.

How much easier can it get?

---

9   Genesis 1:26
10   Temanite—a man from Yemen in Hebrew.

৵৹৵

Tool: A Vision That Sustains Life

The Bible is non-compromising about the need to have a personal vision for life: *Where there is no vision, the people perish:* (Proverbs 29:18).

People, who lack a mental image for their life, die. This last verse sounds quite ominous. Is this only a literary biblical threat or is there some truth to that?

KEY CONCEPT:

Every person must have a unique vision for their life.

Like many other statements in the Bible, this verse has present day explanation. A person with no vision is likely despondent and depressed. Depressed patients often lose their appetite and lose weight. Prolonged weight loss often leads to malnutrition. A state of malnutrition leads to depressed immunity and hence susceptibility to infections. Further, it leads to lower resistance to randomly circulating mutated new cancer cells.

The individual mental image is a purpose or a meaning that a person gives to his or her life. This purpose becomes a goal or objective to be pursued. Where there is meaning to life—there is life. The power, the forces and momentum of the LOA will go into effect and move the visionary person towards fulfillment of this objective. It is an inherent human behavioral trait.

Caution: be certain that your vision is productive, beneficial and life sustaining for yourself and for others. Visions of catastrophe are as likely to manifest to the dreamer, as are visions of benestrophe.

৵৹৵

Dr. Viktor E. Frankl (1905–1997) was a renowned psychiatrist and neurologist from Vienna Austria. He was incarcerated during World War II in Nazi concentration camps including Auschwitz and Dachau.

After his liberation in his landmark book, *Man's Search for Meaning*, Dr. Frankl describes a fellow inmate who had a dream of being liberated on March 30, 1945. When March twenty-nine came and went the inmate, "F. suddenly became ill and ran high temperature... On March thirtieth, the day his prophesy had told him that the war and suffering would be over for him, he became delirious and lost consciousness. On March thirty-first he was dead."[11] This inmate had no longer reason to live and he was "liberated" by his death in the wrong way.

Dr. Frankl was liberated from the concentration camp on April 27, 1945. He later developed his life lessons from the concentration camps into a theory known as *Logotherapy* and a method of psychological therapy known as Existential Psychotherapy.

---

11   Viktor E. Frankl, MD, PhD: Man's Search for Meaning, Beacon Press, Boston MA. 2006. P.75. First published in German in 1946.

PART TWO

THE MASTER
ATTRACTORS

Chapter Two

MOSES A MASTER
OF THE LAW OF
ATTRACTION

The story of Moses' origins is first told in Exodus Chapter 2. It is probable that he lived around 1300–1400 BCE. Moses was adopted by the Egyptian royal court of the Pharaoh. He grew up in the royal court and was educated there. The New Testament, authored several hundred years after the writing of the book of Exodus, reveals more details about Moses' background and youth. *"And Moses was learned in all the wisdom of the Egyptians and was mighty in words and deeds."* (Acts 7:22). Moses became a man of higher consciousness due to his early life background among Egypt's royals. Much of Moses' education was acquired from the rich Egyptian culture and sciences. *"And when he was full forty years old it came into his heart to visit his brethren the children of Israel."*[12] The book of Acts provides more information about Moses as an intellectually powerful man. That is because the Greek origins of the book of Acts is thought to be in (60–69 CE). The authors may have been or were in fact familiar with three or four older Greek language versions of the Hebrew Bible. Those old Greek versions were authored in Egypt before the classic

---

12   Acts 7:23

21

translation known as the Septuagint that was state sponsored around 250 BCE by Ptolemy, the Hellenic King of Egypt. The extant Hebrew language versions of the TANACH do not allude to the notion that Moses *"was learned in all the wisdom of the Egyptians..."* This is in line of Judaic tradition maintaining that Moses was exclusively a Hebrew-Judaic prophet who was uninfluenced by Egyptian or non-Israelite doctrines.

∽⑥↝

Once Moses went to visit his brethrens, his life changed. He took on the leadership of the children of Israel for the next eighty years of his life.

MOSES — A LEADER WITH A VISION

Moses the great biblical prophet, leader-politician, lawgiver and healer was a master practitioner of the LOA.

Moses as he is described in the Hebrew Bible demonstrated in his life acts of leadership, and ethical teachings. Moses used the LOA to reach his goals and objectives. He held great visions in front of him. Moreover, the essence of his visions was repeatedly inscribed in writing onto stone tablets. Next, he utilized and applied the power of the human emotions to sell his followers on his visions. His greatest objective was to create the Hebrew nation out of the Egyptians' slaves. Next he used the power of emotions to convince the Egyptian Pharaoh and his political power players in the Egyptian court and compelled them to cooperate reluctantly with him to achieve his objectives. Throughout this book, we come back to various episodes in Moses' work and highlight his tools while practicing the Key Concepts of the LOA.

∽⑥↝

The burning bush in the desert of Midian in the Sinai Peninsula was the first vision Moses experienced. The Bible tells us of this vision:

> *"And the angel of the Lord appeared unto him in a flame of fire out of the midst of a bush: and he looked, and, behold, the bush burned with fire, and the bush was not consumed.*

And Moses said, I will now turn aside, and see this great sight, why the bush is not burnt. And when the Lord saw that he turned aside to see, God called unto him out of the midst of the bush, and said Moses, Moses. And he said, Here I am." (Exodus 3:2–4).

The importance of having a vision as a prime Key Concept for manifestation by means of the LOA will be explained and referred repeatedly again.

There are two important points in this momentous historical and theological tradition. First is the nature of the physical vision by Moses who was a human being. The second is the theological implications of this vision. Let me examine the first point.

What was the nature of the eternal flame that Moses saw? Could it be that there was a burning entity in the Sinai desert? The answer is emphatically yes. The Sinai Peninsula is to the present day a source for crude oil and natural gas. There are oil wells and natural gas wells in the western part of the Sinai desert and east of the Gulf of Suez. The scene that the Bible tells in the quote above may well have been a continuously burning flame from an underground source of natural gas or crude oil. A second possibility for the incessant flame was volcanic activity. There is no present day evidence that suggests volcanic activity during the biblical times, but there is no reason to exclude this possibility. The Sinai is part of the geologic fault line known as the African-Syrian fault.

The second point in the story as quoted—is the vision of encountering the Divine. This was a subjective personal experience by Moses that does not require "scientific" validation. The point is that the vision inspired Moses and compelled him to start acting on his visionary convictions. From here on Moses felt driven to act in alignment with his vision to achieve the major objectives of articulating the existence of a monotheistic God and liberating the Children of Israel from slavery in Egypt to a state of national freedom in the Land of Canaan.

We refer to this landmark event in Moses' life and his subsequent behavior as a prime example of taking *"inspired action."* In the course of these events he gave the Children of Israel a new set of laws known as the Torah or the Five Books of Moses (Pentateuch), while delivering them from Egyptian slavery.

Moses was an alumnus of the Egyptian court of the Pharaohs. The Egyptian civilization in the 14th century BCE is known to have been highly developed in the sciences of astronomy, engineering and architecture. The great pyramids in Egypt are testimony to the architectural and engineering capabilities of the Egyptians. Written documents from this period were discovered, and translated to contemporary languages and are available for scholarly studies.[13] Moses was adept in the established culture and civilization of Egypt during his period. This culture includes the emergence of a monotheistic theological doctrine.[14]

Experiencing a vision and holding the vision in the mind's eye is the first driving mental force that triggers the Law of Attraction into action.

Recall that the human mind operates through collaborative and associative thoughts. Therefore, any mental vision—expressed or unexpressed replicates itself and summons the external matching conditions required to manifest the vision.

EFFECTIVE TOOL: WRITING DOWN THE VISION

This is seemingly a simple tool. The act of writing down a thought, describing a vision in a form of a design, stating a goal, or saying a prayer—all virtually advance the manifesting of the mental content into reality. Moses, who was an early master of the LOA and a great manifestor in the Bible, employed the powerful tool of writing his vision to guarantee its transformation from the mental phase into an empiric everyday reality.

---

13   In 1887 in an archeological discovery was made in El-Amarna, Egypt. Over 300 tablets written in cuneiform symbols of the Acadian language that reflect the life, politics and business of the then ruling 18th dynasty in Egypt. El-Amarna seems to have been a central city in the civilization of the ruling Pharaoh during the Mosaic era.

14   This monotheistic view was introduced in Egypt in the 14th century BCE by the then ruling Pharaoh known as Akhenaton.

MOSES GIVES THE LAW IN WRITING

Moses was a Law-Giver. As such, he was instructed by his deity that the Law must be stated and given in writing:

> *"And the lord said unto Moses, Write thou these words: for after the tenor of these words I have made a covenant with thee and with Israel. And he was there with the Lord forty days and forty nights; he did neither eat bread, nor drink water. And he wrote upon the tables the words of the covenant, the Ten Commandments."* (Exodus 34:27–28).

JOSHUA HAD A WRITTEN "THINGS TO DO" LIST

Moses had an administrative officer whom he trained, and who later became his successor and political heir. His name was Joshua.

In the Bible, the purpose of writing things down is expressed in the following directive: *"And the Lord said unto Moses, Write this for a memorial in a book and rehearse it in the ears of Joshua..."* Exodus 17:14.

Smile: creating a "To Do" list is a very old practice. About 3,300 years old. Joshua, who was Moses' administrative assistant had to comply with this practice.

KEY CONCEPT:
Write down your vision and goals.

THE POWER OF THE WRITTEN WORD

In the following chapters we deal with the practice of writing down your "stuff" as a tool for attracting and manifesting. The importance of writing down the intent or the desired outcome of a mental bidding, as a Key Concept in the practice of the LOA cannot be overemphasized.

The importance of memorializing things in writing recurs all along the biblical narrative:

> *"And he gave unto Moses, when he had made an end of communing with him upon Mount Sinai, **two tables of testimony, tables of stone, written with the finger of God.**"* (Exodus 31:18).

Later we are told: *"And the Lord said unto Moses, **Write thou these words**: for after the tenor these words I have made **a covenant** with thee and with Israel."* (Exodus 34:27).

This last verse is a testimony of millennia old, uninterrupted practice, that a—contractual agreement must be inscribed in writing.

Moreover—a written covenant transforms the agreement into a reality.

Here is a modern day advice. After you have written down your intent or goal you set to yourself—do something small about it. Do something small and seemingly insignificant as it may be, towards manifesting your objective. Make a phone call. Do an internet search. Consult a trusted friend on how to proceed. Cut and paste on your wall a photo or diagram of your object.

Just do it.

THINK WITH CLARITY

In the book of Proverbs, we find plainly stated:

For as he thinketh in his heart, so is he: (Proverbs 23:7)

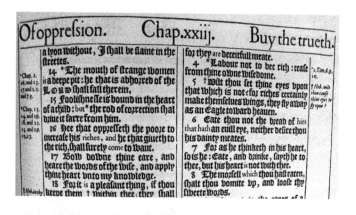

Proverbs 23:7 in a facsimile of the King James Bible 1611

This verse inspired the British author James Allen. He became known for his book (1902): *As a Man Thinketh.* In his book, Allen states that *man is literally, what he thinks, his character being the complete sum of all his thoughts.*

The same verse seems to have inspired Earl Nightingale to record his audio message *The Strangest Secret.* In that inspirational classic, he coined the phrase: *"We become what we think about".*[15]

LESSONS FROM MODERN HISOTRY

On August 28, 1963, the Reverend Martin Luther King stood on the steps of the Lincoln Memorial in Washington DC and orated his historical speech, "I Have a Dream." The speech gave the impetus for the Civil Rights Legislation by the U.S. Congress. Dr. King also said: *"I have a dream that my four little children will one day live in a nation where they will not be judged by the color of their skin, but by the content of their character."* Today, two young black girls are residing in the White House in Washington DC as members of the First Family. It took the will and power of millions of Americans grouped together to make this dream a reality. While Dr. King is gone, his vision endures and expands in present reality.

> **KEY CONCEPT:**
> The LOA provides limitless channels for manifestation.

Such is the power of a visionary declaration of a dream to change a nation.

On June 12, 1987, U.S. president Ronald Reagan delivered a speech at the Brandenburg Gate by the Berlin wall. In that speech President Reagan challenged Mr. Gorbachev, the chief of the Communist Party of the Soviet

---

15 Earl Nightingale: The Strangest Secret. Simple Truth LLC/Nightingale–Conant. 2005. Naperville, Illinois.

Union: *"Mr. Gorbachev, open this gate. Mr. Gorbachev, tear down this wall!"* On November 9, 1989, Berlin residents from both sides of the wall started to chip the wall and tear it down. It required the might of the United States people, economy and military technology to change the historical reality in Europe and bring down the Berlin wall.

Such was the power of the spoken words uttered in public by one man to change the course of European history.

Each oratorical declaration of vision and objective served as a trigger that attracted infinite influences that coalesced together to change history and manifest a new desired outcome.

RESPECT THE POWER OF YOUR THOUGHTS

The LOA operates both ways—positive or negative. That means it will support the manifesting of any mental picture or expressed wish. If your thoughts are negative or if you are fearful, the LOA will manifest your fears or the undesirable circumstance you are afraid of. The LOA is non-judgmental. A negative thought replicates after itself in the mind as does a positive thought. A thought of catastrophe expands in the mind and draws to the negative thinker collateral thoughts and manifests circumstances of catastrophe. The biblical book of wisdom—Job—had this figured out. There Job says: *For the thing which I greatly feared is come upon me, and that which I was afraid of is come unto me.* (Job 3:25).

A person cannot hold two thoughts—opposite of each other—and expect the thoughts to manifest. Opposite thoughts cause mental confusion and annul each other. The LOA manifests any circumstance—whether you wish it or abhor it. Therefore, clear thinking can sometimes mean—life or death.

Let us repeat—visions of catastrophe are as likely to manifest to the thinker, as are visions of benestrophe. So clear thinking of beneficent life and a clear unwavering mental picture of munificent living is a requirement for manifesting best results.

One more contemporary example: A joint persistent and resolved intent or goal shared by friends or partners delivers powerful results. It works phenomenally for partners of two. My friends and colleagues are a married couple. For several years, they had no children. Visits with reputable fertility experts did not seem to get them closer to their aspiration of enlarging their family circle.

After careful reflection, my friends decided to do what was under their control—expand their family by adopting a baby. They were happy with their adopted son. In their happiness, they went ahead and adopted a second baby. Their family grew further and their joy multiplied. Shortly after that, my friend became pregnant and gave birth to a baby boy. Later she gave birth to a second boy. Altogether, they are today the proud parents of four adult men.

> **KEY CONCEPT:**
> Begin where you are by acting in alignment with your vision.

My friends had a clear vision. They acted in alignment with their desires. They did what they could to manifest their desires. They did not waver. They acted in the direction of their dreams of the perfect family they envisioned. The unfathomable forces of the universe joined them to manifest their perfect vision.

A Powerful Tool: The Mastermind Alliance

The mastermind alliance also known as a *brain trust* is a group of friendly, cooperative persons who fire up their intellectual prowess together for the purpose of achieving a common goal. Napoleon Hill used the term *"mastermind alliance"* in his writings. This tool was utilized by the tycoons of industry in nineteenth century America. Rulers in history relied on mastermind alliance to do their bidding. President Franklyn D. Roosevelt used a brain trust of academicians to advance his New Deal policy. President John F. Kennedy had an inner brain trust consisting of his brother Robert and the renowned counselor Clark Clifford. In some countries, it is called a war cabinet and in some corporations, an executive committee. The purpose is the same—to pool the brightest ideas in support of manifesting a common goal or a vision. Husband and wife commonly make up together a brain trust of two.

❧ ❧

In a previous example, we saw how overcoming the barrier of sterility by married couples is a common goal. Manifesting an expanded family by a childless couple is a mastermind alliance by the married couple who share the same goal.

There are usually additional members to this mastermind alliance in the form of fertility experts and obstetricians. All are laboring as a team to manifest the joyous precious outcome. More demonstrations of breaking the barrier of infertility come later in this chapter.

❧ ❧

Moses Utilized A Mastermind Alliance

The members of his mastermind group consisted of his circle of family and seventy tribal elders-trustees. His inner circle included his brother Aaron, his sister Miriam and his father-in-law Jethro. His administrative assistant—Joshua—was an integral member of his mastermind group. The purpose of Moses' mastermind alliance was to get the Children of Israel to the Promised Land—the Land of Canaan.

A wider mastermind alliance that supported Moses was formed by a Divine directive. *"And the Lord said unto Moses, Gather unto me seventy men of the elders of Israel, whom thou knowest to be the elders of the people, and officers over them; and bring them unto the tabernacle of the congregation, that they may stand there with thee."* (Numbers 11:16). The consultative function of the seventy elders can also be inferred from their presence at important discussions where subsequent responsibilities for the governance of the people were shared under this Divine directive: *"And I will come down and talk with thee there and I will take of the spirit which is upon thee, and will put it upon them; and they shall bear the burden of the people with thee, that thou bear it not thyself alone."* (Numbers 11:17).

The elders of Israel acted as the ruling rank in addition to holding consultations with Moses. *"And Moses called unto them; and Aaron and all the rulers of the congregation returned unto him: and Moses talked with them."* (Exodus 34:31).

If you want to emulate the wisdom of King Solomon—acquire the benefits derived from utilizing a mastermind alliance and partner with people who are loyal and supportive of your vision.

King Solomon, the traditional author of the book of Ecclesiastes, had the mastermind alliance in mind when he wrote: *"Two are better than one; because they have a good reward for their labour."* (Ecclesiastes 4:9). Later he adds: *"...and a threefold cord is not quickly broken."* (Ecclesiastes 4:12). The implication is that a mastermind group consisting of three partners is better than a mastermind of just two persons. Chapter Three of this book is dedicated to King Solomon—the grand master of the LOA. It brings more essentials and quotes numerous verses on masterminding with partners to implement joint ventures.

KEY CONCEPT:
Engage and utilize a Mastermind Alliance.

Tool: The Focus Group

The focus group is a modern derivative tool of the master mind alliance. A *focus group* is a research instrument in qualitative social and psychological research in which a group of people are asked about their perceptions, opinion and attitude toward an idea, a goal, a service or a product. The participants are encouraged to speak out their mind and express any opinion or feeling they may harbor. The sponsor of the focus group gains insight to the mental status and innovative ideas of numerous participants who interact and stimulate each other's thinking.

The focus group tool was initiated by the psychologist Dr. Ernest Dichter and was implemented in applied social studies by Professor Robert

K. Merton. As noted earlier Robert K. Merton introduced also the concept of *self-fulfilling prophecy*.

THE PHENOMENON OF SYNCHRONICITY

The phenomenon of *synchronicity* in human events is claimed by many authors as a facilitation tool or a channel for accomplishing desired objectives.

What is *synchronicity*? It is a coincidence of *seemingly* related occurrences while they are *causally unrelated*. The occurrences are meaningfully related and promoted *as if* there is a cause and effect relation between the two events by the observers' minds. If two persons are involved in the "synchronous" event, then a perceived causality may be assigned in the thoughts of the two persons.

The prophet Amos made a reference to the concurrence of *synchronicity* in human events when he asked: *"Can two walk together, except they be agreed?"* (Amos 3:3). Regardless of the validity of *synchronicity* as real, (yet non-causally related phenomenon), it occurs because of the heightened awareness of the thinker towards the manifestation of her or his intention.[16]

TOOL: SERENDIPITY

Serendipity[17] is the propensity to make fortuitous (favorable) discoveries while looking for something unrelated.

The phenomenon of *serendipity* is credited with the birth of many innovative ideas and scientific inventions. All thinkers and scientists agree that the mind has to be *primed, prepared and ready to find and manifest the objective*

---

16 The Swiss psychiatrist, C.G. Jung who defined synchronicity as "temporally coincident occurrences of causal events," is a case in point, demonstrating the LOA. He observed a phenomenon, ascribed to it a meaning, gave it a definition and collected evidence for the validity of the concept of synchronicity. The more evidence he collected the more he grew convinced that synchronicity is a true phenomenon. He published his observations and conclusions in book format as a fact supporting his archetypes theory. In the process, he created another example of the LOA in action. He attracted evidence to solidify the concept of synchronicity, which he regarded as a truth. This anecdote does not detract from the possible extant reality of synchronicity.

17 The word *serendipity* is derived from a fairy tale about the three princes of Serendip. *Swarnadweep* is a Persian name of the island of Sri Lanka.

without cognitive prejudice. This last sentence implies that a priori thought has already occurred in the mind of the thinker. Further, this nested thought sparked multiple associated thoughts that are on the look-out for a stated goal or objective. The mind was thus primed to attract matching components for the purpose of manifesting the goal or objective.

The most thorough scientific information on the phenomenon of *serendipity* is found in Professor Robert K. Merton's book, *The Travels and Adventures of Serendipity.*[18] It is Professor Robert. K. Merton who coined in 1968 the term *self-fulfilling prophecy* (discussed in Part One of this book). He was awarded the U.S. National Medal of Science for his work (and twenty honorary doctoral degrees along the way).

Taken together, I can speculate that Professor Robert K. Merton (as is his son Robert C. Merton[19]) was a skilled intellectual beneficiary of the Law of Attraction, even though he is not known to have used this term.

∽⥈⥈∾

In conclusion, the phenomena of synchronicity and serendipity, consciously or subconsciously, are enabling tools for manifestation that fall under the framework of the LOA.

Fourteen centuries BCE, the Children of Israel, wandering in the wilderness of the Sinai desert, started to "murmur" (i.e., complain), against their leadership—Moses and Aaron. Their grievance was lack of sufficient food and outright hunger. A certain mental communication (prayer) ensued between Moses and his deity.

KEY CONCEPT:

The LOA manifests through infinite springs of abundance.

Then said the Lord unto Moses, Behold, I will rain bread from heaven for you, and the people shall go out and gather a certain rate every day, that I may prove them... And the Lord spake unto Moses, saying, I have heard the murmurings of the children

---

18   Robert K. Merton and Elinor Barber: The Travels and Adventures of Serendipity. Princeton University Press 2004.

19   Robert K. Merton is the father of Robert C. Merton, a Nobel memorial prize laureate in economics 1997.

of Israel… And it came to pass, that in the evening the quails came up and covered the camp: and in the morning the dew lay round about the host. And when the dew that lay was gone, behold upon the face of the wilderness there lay a small round thing, as small as the hoar frost on the ground. And when the children of Israel saw it they said one to another, It is manna: for they wist not what it was… (Exodus 16:1–15).

Note first, the mental activity that took place in the form of prayer. It is a revelatory communication between Moses and God—preceding the provision of food. Second, the beneficiaries received fare, some of it familiar and some was a new kind of food that they did not expect. They received quails and they received *manna*.

Once again, the LOA brings vast, boundless and unexpected resolution to the state of our wanting, beyond our limited human expectations.

Chapter Three

SOLOMON AND HIS MASTERMIND ALLIANCES

The authors and editors of the Hebrew Bible gave the credit to King Solomon for three books of wisdom: Proverbs, Ecclesiastes and the Song of Songs. In the Bible, Solomon is considered as the wisest man of his time. The wisdom and counsel of loyal spouses, friends, and business partners is a requirement for success according to King Solomon. The principle of the mastermind alliance is a thread that continuously weaves through the Book of Proverbs.

King Solomon was born in 1011 BCE. He lived eighty years and reigned as the King of Israel for 40 years (971–931 BCE). Solomon was the fourth son to his father David. He ascended to the throne after successful political maneuvers and intrigues inside the court involving his mother and a court prophet called Nathan. Solomon was a philanderer having had many (hundreds) wives and concubines.

Solomon chose wisdom over riches. Subsequently he gained riches as a byproduct of his wisdom. The Bible in I Kings 3:5–13 tells the story of how Solomon became the wisest and the richest man of his time. Not coincidentally,

King Solomon had a vision *"in a dream by night."*[20] In his dream he asked of God: *"Give therefore thy servant an understanding heart to judge thy people, that I may discern between good and bad: for who is able to judge this thy so great a people?"* (I Kings 3:9).

Because King Solomon had no other request of God in his vision, God granted him his wish and a bonus: *"And I have also given thee that which you thou hast not asked, both riches and honour: so that there shall not be any among the kings like unto thee all thy days."* (I Kings 3:13).

The biblical account of Solomon makes a point:

> *"And the God gave Solomon wisdom, and understanding exceedingly much, and largess of the heart, even as the sand that is on the sea shore. And Solomon's wisdom excelled the wisdom of all the children of the east country, and all the wisdom of Egypt. For he was wiser than all men…"* (I Kings 4:29-31).[21]

THE MASTERMIND OF COUNSELORS

The cornerstone of the teachings of Solomon in the book of Proverb is the acquisition of knowledge and wisdom. *"He that getteth wisdom loveth his soul: he that keepeth understanding shall find food."* (Proverbs 18:8).

Gaining of wisdom and knowledge is accomplished through the input of advisors and mentors. *"Without counsel purposes are disappointed: but in the multitude of counselors they are established."* (Proverbs 15:22).

Solomon admonishes his reader: *"… in the multitude of counselors there is safety."* (Proverbs 11:14).

Further, *"He that walketh with wise men shall be wise…"* (Proverbs 13:20).

There are many methods to acquire wisdom from counselors. Reliance on a council of advisors is one method. The council of advisors is a mastermind alliance. Solomon had a rounded cabinet of ministers that were responsible for matters of military, treasury (taxes), priesthood, and scribes.[22]

---

20 I Kings 3:5
21 This categorical statement about Solomon's wisdom is quoted in the Hebrew Bible version in I kings 5:9-11.
22 I Kings 4:1-7

Solomon learned from his father, King David, to rely on counselors' advice. David had his own coterie of counselors and scribes that kept records of the monarchic transactions. *"Also Jonathan David's uncle was a counselor, a wise man and a scribe"*.[23] David had additional other counselors and utilized a mastermind alliance. In addition, he maintained archival records taken by scribes. The royal decrees were preserved in writing for future reference and posterity. Included were David's philosophical thoughts and poetic ideas. His collected musings were canonized in the book of Psalms.

INTERNATIONAL ALLIANCES

A method of engaging and neutralizing one's potential competitors and adversaries is marrying into their family. *"Solomon made affinity with Pharaoh, King of Egypt, and took Pharaoh's daughter, and brought her into the city of David"*.[24] Marriages between royal families were practiced throughout history and are common in European royal courts. Marriages among royalties serve two purposes: maintaining the aura of noble exclusivity and at the same time mitigating the chance of international wars.

Social networking among the royals is a repeated method in Solomon's portfolio of political tactics. Flirting with the ruler of the opposite gender— the queen of Sheba[25] in this case—is another method that Solomon employed. He impressed the queen who arrived in Jerusalem accompanied by a heavy caravan of camels loaded with presents, spices, gold, and jewels. She *"communed with him of all that was in her heart"*.[26] The queen of Sheba was impressed by Solomon and the grandeur of his household and more.[27] The fine details of the relationship between King Solomon and Queen of Sheba is not reported in the Bible.[28]

---

23 I Chronicles 27:32
24 I Kings 3:1
25 The Land of Sheba is thought to be the present day Arabian Peninsula.
26 I Kings 10:2
27 "And King Solomon gave to the queen of Sheba all her desire, whatsoever she asked…" II Chronicles 9:12.
28 Ethiopian tradition claims that Solomon fathered with Queen of Sheba a son—Menelik I who went on to become the founder of the dynasty that ruled Ethiopia for 2,900 years and ended with King Haile Selassie in 1974.

In his political and imperial wisdom, Solomon managed to establish an international treaty with the ruler to the north of his kingdom—Hiram, King of Tyre. King Hiram provided the lumber and cut stones to build Solomon's temple in Jerusalem.[29] As noted, King Hiram (Huram) kept written correspondence with King Solomon.[30]

Altogether, Solomon created alliances with the rulers surrounding his country—Tyre to the north, Sheba to the south and Egypt to the southwest. He benefited from the prosperity of peace and skillfully constructed the great capital of Jerusalem.

The Bible in I Kings 10:24, is explicit about Solomon's wisdom: *"And all the earth sought to Solomon, to hear his wisdom, which god had put in his heart."*

NATIONAL PROSPERITY THROUGH THE LOA

The books of Chronicles make twice the point that King Solomon *prospered.*[31] Whatever methods of success that Solomon employed returned to him in the form of prosperity and abundance[24]. The Hebrew Bible tells us that Solomon shared his success methods with future generations in the form of the books of wisdom attributed to his authorship—Proverbs, Ecclesiastes and Song of Songs.

We cite repeatedly in this volume the LOA Key Concept, from Proverbs 23:7:

For as he thinketh in his heart—so is he.

It is of significance that two of the cornerstone concepts of the LOA are attributed to King Solomon—thinking up a vision of the desired reality and utilizing a mastermind alliance with wise people.

---

29   I kings chapter 5.
30   II Chronicles 2:11—*"Then Huram the king of Tyre answered in writing, which he sent to Solomon..."*
31   I Chronicles 29:23 and II Chronicles 7:11.

Chapter Four

A MASTER REALTOR CALLED JABEZ

T he Bible tells a story of a man whose name was Jabez[32] (*Jaabetz* or phonetically read *Yaabetz* in Hebrew).

He is introduced as a man who *was more honorable than his brethren.* We are told also that the family of Jaabetz made a living as scribes[33]— they were writers. The significance of Jabez being a son to a family of scribes will be made clear later.

> *Jabez called on the God of Israel, blesse me indeede, and enlarge my coast, and that thine hand might bee with me and that wouldest keepe mee from evill that it may not grieve me...*[34] Sure enough, *God granted him that which he requested.* (I Chronicles 4:9–10).

---

32 ιαβεσ in the Greek version of the Septuagint.
33 I Chronicles 2:55—*And the families of the scribes which dwelt at Jabez.*
34 Note the 16th century English spelling style. See the text in the following original folio from the KJV 1611.

It is likely that Jabez was aware of the LOA—Ask and Receive that which is given. The Bible tells us that Jabez asked ("*called on the God of Israel*"), and received ("*God granted him that which he requested*").

The Bible does not say that he "prayed"—it says that he just *called on the God of Israel.* How many times did Jabez repeat his request (or prayer?). We are not told that he repeated his *call.*

It is tempting to speculate that he may have written down his request, or taken creative action of some sort. Jabez may have acted in the service of God.

It is possible that he did not do anything other than getting ready to receive that which he asked. The Bible does not advise us of any details.

The Bible does not disclose what Jabez did during the time interval between his Asking and Receiving. What Jabez did or did not do remains the *secret* of the Bible—a *secret* of a different kind.[35]

In line with this possibility that Jabez did not do anymore other than ask and receive, the post-modern teachers of the LOA maintain that in order to manifest a want or a wish it may be sufficient for the person to declare an intent, or set a goal and in due course receive (achieve) it. The required condition is to *believe* that the intent, or goal, or prayer request, is now manifested or will manifest—at its own time and on its own accord. The petitioner must stay in a mental state of heightened awareness and readiness to take inspired action, if indicated, and receive the request or petition.

What was the nature of Jabez' request? Jabez voiced a four parts request: He asked for God's general blessing.

Second, he asked that his *coast*[36] (border) be enlarged. The NKJV states that his *territory* be enlarged.

Thirdly, he asked metaphorically that "God's hand" will guide him.

Lastly, he asked that he will be protected from evil.

"*And god granted him that which he requested.*"

Jabez got the extra territory he asked for. Talk about success in real estate...

---

35   Psalm 25:14—*The secret of the Lord is with them that fear him; and he will shew them his covenant.*

36   The Hebrew text states that he asked for his border to be widened. The Latin Vulgate was translated directly from the Hebrew Bible by St. Jerome who was a talented linguist. The Vulgate version reads *dilataveris terminos* meaning *widen the border.* Jabez asked to acquire more land and his wish was granted. It should be noted that *terminus* in English, means also a goal. In ancient Rome Terminus was the deity that presided over borders and landmarks.

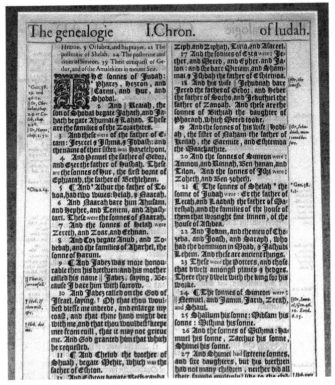

The Prayer of Jabez. I Chronicles 4:9-10.
From an original folio of 1611 King James Bible.

❧❧

The story of Jabez is a compelling account of the Law of Attraction in the Hebrew Bible—bringing abundance and protecting from grief.

The author of Proverbs was familiar with the case history of Jabez and so he concurred: "*The blessing of the Lord it makes rich, and he adds no sorrow with it.*" (Proverbs 10:22). In plain words—success is its own justification.

The book titled, *The Prayer of Jabez,*[37] was on the New York Times #1 best seller list.

Such is the power of the LOA: a gift that keeps on giving—then and now.

---

37 Bruce Wilkinson: The Prayer of Jabez. Multnomah Publishers, Inc. Oregon. 2000.

∽🙂🙂🙂

Is It Necessary To Take Action?

Let us confront the question whether it is necessary to take action in order to manifest. Does the universe need your help?

If you express intent or a wish you are better off writing it down. This is a simple action taken. Many argue that you have to believe that you will receive and do some work towards manifesting your objective. The lesson from the story of Jabez is that it's adequate to ask and then receive. No further action needs to be taken. The reasoning behind the "no further action is needed" after asking is subtle—if you ask and then feel compelled to act, it indicates that you have a doubt whether your request will be fulfilled by the all universal framework of the all-inclusive LOA.

In other words, taking action is an outside indicator of inner doubts that hinder or decelerate the LOA from manifesting the requested objective.

∽🙂🙂🙂

The Law Of Attraction Is Available To All

Let us move on to a different area of life where the LOA works its seemingly "miraculous" manifestations.

The state of deep prayer or meditation is conducive to manifesting a wish, solving a specific need or satisfying a state of want.

∽🙂🙂🙂

Hannah was the wife of Elkanah. She did not bear him children. In her anguish, she went along with her husband on a pilgrimage to the temple of God in Shiloh. There in her bitterness of soul she prayed unto the Lord and wept. She asked God to remember her and give her a child. *She spoke in her heart; only her lips moved, but her voice was not heard* (I Samuel 1:13). The priest Eli who was present there, *answered and said, Go in peace: and the God of Israel grant thee thy petition that thou hast asked of him* (1:17). By next year Hannah had a son who was named Shemuel (Samuel), meaning God hears (prayers).

This story illustrates two points. First, it is sufficient, oftentimes, to hold a mental image of the desired outcome. It is not required to verbalize it loudly; nor is it necessary to write it down, although all these activities are mutually supportive. Second, a wish or intent expressed while in an intense emotional state of mind is a powerful trigger of the LOA into manifestation.

This and other stories demonstrate that prayer while holding a mental picture of a perfect state of health facilitates healing and brings about the desired state of health and wellness.[38] In this case the state of wellness is—a fertile marital union.

⋘⋙

In the story of Hannah and Elkanah—the prayer of supplication is a focused form of mental intent to bear children. The Bible is clear on the nature of that intent. That intent takes the form of a promise (fulfilled under certain conditions): *"...And I will take sickness away from the midst of thee. There shall nothing cast their young, nor be barren, in thy land."* (Exodus 23:25–26).[39]

⋘⋙

My friend and colleague is a physician in medical practice. He is a Muslim who is married. The couple had no children. After about two years into the marriage, the couple embarked on a pilgrimage to Mecca. They pursued the Muslim tradition and rituals. They returned home after one month. His head was shaven of hair. Nine months later my friend's wife gave birth to *triplets*— two girls and a boy who are now nine years old.

Abundance means prosperity in all areas of life—material riches and generations of offspring. The LOA does not discriminate between persons of different creeds.

> KEY CONCEPT:
> The LOA operates by inclusion. It does not discriminate.

---

38 Psalm 30:2—*O Lord my God I cried unto thee, and thou hast **healed** me.*

39 The words *"cast their young,"* means in modern English—miscarriage of pregnancy.

Esther Hicks said it best in one of her legendary workshops on the Law of Attraction:

"There is no exclusion in an attraction based universe. There is only inclusion."

No living person is excluded from their share of success, health and abundance.

When I was required by my health insurance carrier to select a primary care physician, guess whom I chose as my physician?

I regard with great esteem people who demonstrated in their own life that they live in alignment with the Law of Attraction. I gravitate towards these folks because they radiate a charisma of irresistible success.

Chapter Five

MASTER HEALERS IN GENERAL PRACTICE

ATTRACTING HEALTH

Good health can be attracted. Healing and cure can be attracted by a sick person who desires recovery and wellness. The Bible tells numerous stories involving prophets and visionaries who delivered demonstrations of healing and recovery from diseases.

Ask any healthcare professional and she or he will agree that the first requirement for medical recovery is the patient's will to heal. Furthermore, the patient must have a will to survive. The journey to healing and cure may be long and painful for the patient. That means holding the vision of healing and cure with unshakable faith for long periods of time.

The LOA fundamentals for manifesting health include:

A *will* to enjoy good health—an intention to live healthy;

A *vision*—a mental picture of good health in the mind's eye of the patient;

A *support system* for promoting healing and rehabilitation—that is a *mastermind alliance*. It consists of the patient and her or his health team. The health team may include any or all of the following: world-class doctors, specialty-consultants for second opinion, specialized nurses, pastoral care practitioners, and a prayer group.

Lastly, the patient must bear a firm belief that the cure is on the way!

These elements are involved in most cases of a successful medical recovery and cure. As a rule, the more complicated the patient's medical condition is, the greater is the requirement for the visible presence of the framework of the LOA (see Key Concepts). A case in point—a healthcare provider cannot help a patient with cancer to experience a remission or a cure if the patient does not want treatment.

In the previous pages, several elements of the LOA were listed and discussed and regardless of the current mainstream clinical terminology—all those elements in whatever terms the reader selects to use—must be present in order to effect a remission or cure. The professional jargon is not the critical element. The mental state of awareness of the patient is instrumental. The patient's ability to incorporate elements of the LOA into the plan of care is conducive towards healing and cure. When the right mental attitude is present, then creative action of cure follows.

Let it be clear—first class healthcare providers, world-class healthcare facilities, and cutting edge medicines are solid components of the framework of LOA when it is applied to attracting health.

⋘⋙

ENVISIONING THE CURE

The Bible goes back to the first Hebrew prophet and law-giver—Moses, (1400 BCE), and describes a case of a mass poisoning from desert snake-bites. There are recognizable elements of the LOA Moses utilized to heal the sick. The snake-bite victims came to Moses, their leader, "asking" him to pray for their recovery. *And Moses prayed for the people,* —at their asking. (Numbers 21:6–9).

> *"And Moses made a serpent of brass, and put it upon a pole, and it came to pass that if a serpent had bitten a man, when he beheld the serpent of brass, he lived."* (Numbers 21:9).

When we look for the elements of the LOA in this biblical story, we find first that the patients came to Moses, the healer, "asking" for help—medical help. Second, Moses prayed. Prayer of intercession is a demonstration of deliberate thinking with intent. Moses directed the patients to view and envision the venomous cause of their poisoning hung on a pole. Once they viewed the cause of their ailment, they were able to manifest their recovery. What is missing from the story is how the serpents were subsequently exterminated... This item remains the secret of the Bible.

Better yet, the use of a serpent hanging from a pole remains customary in our present time—as the symbol for the medical profession—the Aesculapius. Again, success is its own justification...

How patients heal and recover is not always obvious in every case even to contemporary medical scientists. In this era of genomic medicine and gene therapy, there are still many disease entities that remain without cure. Nonetheless, there is something built-in within the human organism that enhances its spontaneous ability to self-heal in many instances. See the case of seasonal influenza outbreaks that come and go annually. The influenza virus bypasses many folks while still other folks who contract the virus recover on their own (or with the help of chicken soup). This last comment is to introduce the statement in Exodus 15:23 *"...for I am the Lord that healeth thee."* If that is the case then there is a positive role for prayer and belief to facilitate or enhance the process of healing. Furthermore, the LOA as we now understand it acts smoother and faster under the influence of a decree or a declared intent to recover by the sick patient.

There is a popular belief that the healing and recovery come from the Divine and the healers of the various occupational classes—physicians, nurses, and pastors are only channels to bring about the healing and recovery. That belief is also good enough.

THE GENERAL PRACTICE OF ELIJAH

The stories of Elijah start abruptly in I Kings chapter 17. Elijah is thought to have lived in the ninth century BCE. He is revered by the three great monotheistic religions. This legendary prophet performed two successive manifestations: first, he demonstrated abundance. Next, he manifested healing ("resurrection from death").

Elements of the LOA in action exist in these episodes that are described in I Kings chapters 17–18. A manifestation of abundance (I Kings 17:10–16) came first. Next comes the demonstration of healing and cure by Elijah:

> "...*the son of the woman, the mistress of the house, fell sick; and his sickness was so sore that there was no breath left in him. ... And he said unto her, Give me thy son. And he took him out of her bosom, and carried him up into a loft, where he abode, and laid him upon his own bed. And he cried unto the Lord and said, O Lord my God, hast thou also brought evil upon the widow with whom I sojourn by slaying her son? And he stretched himself upon the child three times, and cried unto the Lord, and said, O Lord my god I pray thee let this child's soul come into him again. And the Lord heard the voice of Elijah and the soul of the child came into him again and he revived...*" (I Kings 17:17–24)

Three Key Concepts of the LOA that are demonstrated in this biblical story.

First, Elijah said an intercessory prayer. A prayer is an act of "asking!"

Second, Elijah took action—an inspired remedial action, a healing action. Elijah started to work under the circumstances given to him.

Third, Elijah started to work on his "case" before he offered the prayer and before he had any assurance from God. Elijah started to heal the child based on his own unwavering belief that *the child will recover.* He started what seems to be an act of CPR first, and dealt with the formality of prayer later!

Lastly, the widow "received" her revived child.

Note that Elijah did not accept any outcome other than a child who is well and alive. He did not negotiate for anything other than *a cure* for the child.

Transferring the child to a hospice facility or administering palliative care were not adequate alternatives for Elijah. Moreover, Elijah treated the child first and prayed later. Unlike contemporary practices, Elijah did not ask for preapproved certificate of treatment from higher powers that may be. Elijah demonstrated that *the LOA operates most effectively when belief and action are implemented when inspired, without hesitation, and instantly.*

PRAYER AS A TOOL FOR ATTRACTING HEALTH

Prayer is an integral component in the toolbox of the practice of the LOA. Prayer works when the LOA is invoked for manifesting abundance, accomplishing a successful venture, or before going safely on uncharted journeys. Prayer is defined as a communion with God or object of worship in a form of petition or entreaty. The person praying can pray for him or herself and can pray an intercessory prayer on behalf of another person. It is clear by the definition that prayer is offered with a certain outcome in mind.

The healing effect of prayer in the Bible is expressed clearly and unambiguously:

> "*O Lord my God, I cried unto thee, and thou hast healed me.*"
> (Psalm 30:2).

Dr. Larry Dossey, in his book, "Healing Words. The Power of Prayer and The Practice of Medicine,"[40] writes: *"Prayer says something incalculably important about who we are and what our destiny may be."*[41]

Prayer for healing and recovery sets a destiny. In this case, the destiny is healing, recovery and cure. Prayer of petition is the "ask" element of the Key Concepts of the LOA. Prayer of intercession also has an "ask" element that emanates from a "mastermind alliance."

---

40   Published by HarperSanFrancisco (HarperCollins Publishers). 1993.
41   P. 6. Italics in original.

Dr. Alexis Carrel was a renowned physician and surgeon. He was awarded the 1912 Nobel Prize in medicine and physiology for his pioneering work on the techniques of sutures and surgical wound sterility. Dr. Carrel, as a surgeon, was much attuned to the importance and helpfulness of prayer in the course of healing sick or wounded patients. In his book titled: "Prayer," Dr. Carrel wrote: *"A doctor who sees a patient give himself to prayer, can indeed rejoice. The calm engendered by prayer is a powerful aid to healing."* [42]

⊷⊶

Dr. Elmer E. Hess, president of the American Medical Association,[43] was in the opinion that *"We must be trained to take into the sickroom more than our scientific skill. We must allay fears, inspire confidence and strengthen the patient's determination to get well."* During an address to an AMA meeting,[44] he spoke about the role of prayer and faith in healing of sick people. Dr. Hess stated, *"Sometimes what we need most in the sickroom is not the medicine we prescribe. It is the faith and hope that we can instill in our patients."*[45]

⊷⊶

Synergystic Tools: The Written Prayer

It is a practice among the seriously ill patients and among their family members to combine prayer with the written word, i.e. to make a prayer request for healing and cure in writing. The written request is entered into a log available in hospital chapels or by the sick making a pilgrimage to a holy site that is reputable to bring about cures. Such a known shrine that draws thousands of pilgrims seeking the cure is in Lourdes, France.[46] Some are placing the written request in cracks between the large stones that make the Wailing Wall in Jerusalem.[47]

---

42 Out of print. Published in 1948 by Moorehouse-Goraham Co., New York.
43 1955–1956.
44 In Atlantic City, NJ, on June 7, 1957.
45 Quoted in, "The Importance of Prayer." Wade Greene, editor. T.S. Denison & Co. Minneapolis. 1958.
46 Alexis Carrel: The Voyage to Lourdes. New York, Harper & Row, 1939.
47 Candidate for the U.S. presidency—Barack Obama entered a written prayer request while he visited the Wailing Wall during his election campaign. While we do not know what his

∾⟨⟩∾

Why Do Biblical Healers Get Sick And Die?

This book is not a treatise in theology. Nor is this a discussion on morals. However, the question begs itself—can't great biblical healers keep on attracting their own health and longevity indefinitely?

The answer is no, they cannot as we well know from historical experience. They do not live forever. They do not live to manifest indefinitely. As humans, they have some shortcomings or internal conflicts that at some point in their life sets them up to fail, and they die under unforeseen circumstances.

Moses complained to the Lord about his dyslexia: *"…but I am slow of speech, and of a slow tongue,"* an apparent disability that repeatedly bothered him. *"And the lord said unto him, Who has made man's mouth? Or who maketh the dumb, or deaf, or the seeing, or the blind? Have not I the Lord?"* (Exodus 4:10–11). Moses was denied his objective to reach in person the Land of Canaan allegedly because of certain transgression he made against his deity. He died of old age outside his Promised Land.

In a similar vein, Jesus, who died on the cross provided a wise answer to a somewhat similar question. The question was asked of Jesus when he passed by a man blind from birth: *"Master, who did sin, this man or his parents?"* The answer was that neither the blind man nor his parents sinned. *"But that the works of God should be made manifest in him."* (John 9:3). In plain words, that is the way it is. Some facts of life are better left alone and need neither reason, nor value judgment, nor are they a suitable subject for theological speculation.

∾⟨⟩∾

St. Luke—Evangelist, Historian, And Physician

Luke of Antioch is a central figure in the New Testament. He was a Greek and an adherent-disciple traveling alongside Paul of Tarsus. Scholars attribute to Luke talents as a historian, painter and a physician. He never married and died probably at age 84. Bible scholars are in a consensus opinion that he is the author of two books: *The Gospel of St. Luke* and *The Acts of the Apostles*. Both books are historical narratives of Jesus and the early apostles in the first century

written prayer request consisted of, he went on to achieve much in his private and public life.

CE of whom he was one among them. The descriptions Luke authored carry historical gravitas.

The evidence that Luke was a physician comes directly from Paul who wrote to the Colossians: *"Luke the beloved physician, and Demas, greet you."* (Col. 4:14).

In the book of Acts, a healing miracle is described by Luke who is both a physician and historian.[48] While visiting in the city of Troas, Paul, Luke and other disciples stayed late at night listening to Paul's preaching.

> *"And there sat in a window a certain young man named Euthychus, being fallen into a deep sleep: and as Paul was long preaching, he sunk down with sleep, and fell down from the third loft, and was taken up dead. And Paul went down, and fell on him, and embracing him said, Trouble not yourselves; for his life is in him...*
>
> *And they brought the young man alive, and were not a little comforted."* (Acts 20:9–10, 12).

Luke the physician describes with relative accuracy a case of sleep apnea. Paul the leader of the disciples touched the young man, who woke up from his hypercapneic somnolence, and he started to breath and "came back to life." This is another serendipitous demonstration of healing by a highly intelligent master. However, if Luke would have been the first to touch the man the outcome would have been the same because this is the cyclical nature of sleep apnea.[49]

Although this episode may be considered an act of "miraculous" healing, it is more likely to have been an episode of higher awareness, relative to the ancient era. Yet to our contemporary minds it is a straight foreword case.

⊰⊱

Before we leave this chapter on attracting health and healing, let me mention the record of Paul as a healer and teacher of "how to"

---

48 Every good physician is also a good historian.
49 The man could have had Pickwickian syndrome—a variant cause of sleep apnea.

pray: *"Rejoice evermore. Pray without ceasing. In everything give thanks..."*
(I Thessalonians 5:16–18).

Stated otherwise:

Rejoice, Pray, Thank.

Isn't that what the LOA all about?

Chapter Six

HABAKKUK IS FOREVER

I n this chapter, we study the teaching of the biblical prophet Habakkuk.

In his short book in the Hebrew Bible, we find a description on how the LOA was practiced by the sages of the biblical era in order to achieve their desired results.

We see how the prophet converted his vision into an action plan. The prophet tells us of the proven elements of the action plan leading from thought, through vision, to a written statement, and next—to reality. Most importantly, as students of the bible, we are taught by the biblical prophet the mind-set and mental awareness that transforms a vision into the empiric reality of daily life.

❦

The biblical prophet Habakkuk lived in Jerusalem. Habakkuk is thought to have been a "staff prophet" in the temple in Jerusalem. He probably wrote his book at the seventh century BCE.[50] He may have been a musician in the

---

50   609-598 BCE

temple. Supporting this idea is the third chapter in the book of Habakkuk that is thought to be a misplaced Psalm.[51]

The prophet Habakkuk was no plain musician. He was a visionary, a critical thinker, and a great one at that. He did not hesitate to express his impatience with God.[52] Nonetheless, the editors of the Bible retained his criticism in the canon.

Habakkuk outlined an action plan that is inclusive and constitutes the best practice of the LOA in the Bible.

Habakkuk writes in the book named after him (Habakkuk 2:1–4):

(Quote)

1. *I will stand upon my watch, & set mee upon the towere and will watch to see what he will say unto me and what I shall answere when I am reproved.*

2. *And the Lord answered me, and said, Write the vision, and make it plaine upon tables that he may runne that readeth it.*

3. *For the vision is yet for an appointed time, but at the end, it shall speak, and not lie: though it tary, wait for it; because it will surely come, it will not tary.*

4. *Behold, his soul, which is lifted up, is not upright in him: but the just shall live by his faith.*

(End of quote).

---

51   Based on the word *"Shigionoth"* in Habakkuk 3:1, which is a term found only once in Psalms. *Segu* in Acadian means a lamentation.

52   Habakkuk 1:1-3

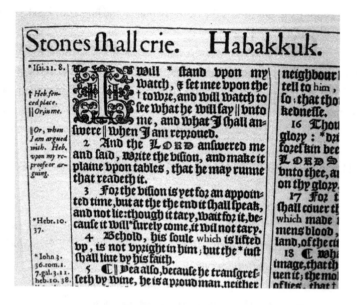

A facsimile of Habakkuk 2:1–4 in King James Bible 1611.
Note the 16th century English spelling style.

THE BEST PRACTICE OF THE LOA IN THE BIBLE

The four verses from the book of Habakkuk (chapter 2), are a proven practice instruction that the Bible offers when it comes to aligning the reader's mind-set, mood and actions with the LOA in order to manifest the desired outcome.

Here is my commentary to what we just read.

A COMMENTARY TO HABAKKUK'S LAW OF ATTRACTION

First verse, tells the person who is seeking to manifest that he or she have to maintain an open mind—listen.

The prophet, Habakkuk, settles on top of a lofty place—a tower. The vistas from lofty places, such as towers, rooftops, ramparts, or mountaintops, always inspire us. Seeking inspiration from a lofty place is not unusual. Centuries later, Peter also went on a housetop and had a trance (a vision).[53]

Habakkuk is a visionary person who watches his internal dialogue. The internal dialogue transpires in the form of an inner voice in the mind's ear. The prophet *lets his thought think about itself*—he watches (tunes in) collateral thoughts and associated thoughts as they are sparked in his mind. This is the meaning of the first verse as it reads: *watch to see what he will say unto me...* "He" (the Divine), will spark ideas in the mind—originating out of the mind's hidden immeasurable stores of infinite knowledge.

These ideas must be given deliberate attention. In these ideas are found the prompts for inspired action. Divinity tells by implication that the visionary thinker has to listen attentively with the mind's ear to what he is about to hear. The explicit action verbs are *set, watch, see* and *answer*. Plenty of mental heavy lifting. It seems that the prophet prepares himself for what we call a brainstorming session.

෴

Second verse is an instruction to exercise the next action item—to write: *Write the vision, and make it plain upon tables that he may run that readeth it.* Wow.

Let us recap. First, there was a vision. Recall Proverbs 29:18—*Where there is no vision, the people perish!* The Prophet had a vision!

So are you: you must first to have a vision.

You can have a vision only for your own life. You cannot hold a vision for another person's life. The vision is about a future event. A vision is not about the past or about the present. The vision must be preserved by writing it down.[54]

෴

---

53 This trance on the housetop turned out later to be a significant landmark in the separation of Christianity from Judaism. "*Peter went up upon a housetop to pray about the sixth hour: And he became very hungry, and would have eaten: but while they made ready, he fell into a trance, And saw heaven opened, and a certain vessel descending unto him, as it had been a great sheet knit at four corners...*" (Acts 10:9–11).
54 A vision may be preserved by a drawing.

Then comes the important action item:

Write down the vision.

My favorite prophet Habakkuk did not have papyri and parchment, nor did he have a plume and ink so his writings were inscribed on clay tablets. The vision, the goal, the intent, the idea must be preserved written on tablets.

When a goal is committed to a written medium, it can and should be revisited—reread, studied and memorized. The goal (intent or vision), has to be written in clear language. The expected outcome must be easy "to run" while reading it, i.e., quickly readable. Present day self-improvement gurus coach us unendingly to write down our personal vision statement and personal goals in the present tense, as if the goal is already manifested.

❧❧

Did you ever hear a promise for freebies to be given to you by an eager silky talking salesperson and you—listened skeptically?

What did you tell the salesperson?

"I want it in writing."

When you were sitting in a job interview and the recruiter mentioned future benefits in addition to the base salary, what was your response?

"Give it to me in writing."

❧❧

Recall the third **Key Concept** of LOA about writing—always get it in writing.

The biblical insistence on writing things reappears in Psalms 45:1–2.

"My heart is inditing a good matter: I speak of the things which I have made touching the king: my tongue is the pen of a ready writer. Thou art fairer than the children of men: grace is poured into thy lips: therefore God hath blessed thee forever."

The Psalmist suggests that expressing (*"inditing"*[55]) a heart-felt sensation of *a good matter* is the target of *the pen of a ready writer.* And the outcome is: *"…therefore God hath blessed thee forever."* It is graceful to speak of a good intention—*a good matter*—but it is much better to write it down using *the pen of a ready writer.*

In alignment with this advice, we write and send personalized greeting cards for the birthdays and anniversaries of our loved ones.[56] If you do that—if you write down your *good matter* feelings of your heart—God will bless *thee* forever.

We each are endowed with prophetic powers. Use your prophetic power—send your family and friends well-wishing or get-well cards as the case may be. Declare them fortunate. Declare them healed.

Amazing grace!

In a previous chapter we already encountered an adept master of manifesting—Jabez. The Bible gives us a clue to Jabez' professional foundation: he was a member of a large family of scribes that dwelt in the town of Jabez.[57] As a scribe, it may well have been his habit to write down his wishes and then receiving that which he asked.

Keeping a prosperity journal or a health journal is fashionable today.[58] It makes you write (*indite*) to yourself—good matters and aspirations, health and wealth.

Third verse of the vision of Habakkuk addresses the element of time: *the vision is yet for an appointed time…wait for it; because it will surely come.*

---

55 *Indite* is an old English word that means to compose or write as a poem.
56 The LOA is a gift that keeps on giving—Hallmark Cards., the largest maker of greeting cards. It operates Over 38,000 retail outlets in the U.S. Employs 12,600 people. Revenue in 2011 was $4.1 Billion.
57 I Chronicle 2:55
58 H.A. Klauser: "Write It down, Make It Happen. Knowing What You Want And Getting it." A Touchstone Book. Simon & Schuster. 2000.

HabakkuK was also a philosopher. He was an early philosopher who wrote between the years 609–598 BCE. HabakkuK is the Hebrew-Judaic contemporary of the Greek, Tales of Miletus, who is considered the first of the pre-Socratic Greek philosophers. They were the teachers of Socrates, Plato and Aristotle who are the trailblazers of the western thought and philosophy (and religion) as we know it.

Here in this verse HabakkuK already tinkered with the relative meaning of time. HabakkuK's full definition of time:

> *"For the vision is yet for an appointed time, but at the end it shall speak, and not lie:* **though it tary wait for it; because it will surly come,** *it will not tary."*

Time is an independent dimension. Time is an illusive subjective concept. For convenience and intellectual laziness we measure time by days or years. But how about assessing (expressing) time in terms of speed of light?

Forget it. It gets too complex...

Therefore HabakkuK's Rule # 3 means that given the right time every vision *will surely come*. Because, given the sum total of circumstances required for manifesting—it has an appointed time. It is that simple.

Now, if you want to witness your vision manifested—do something about it.

Go, write it down... Just write it. Just do it.

Goals, intents and petitions may manifest instantaneously. However, the majority of goals, intents and petitions (the "asking" phase) are manifested ("given") after a time interval between the request and the delivery ("giving" phase). Further, some inspired action may be required by the petitioner during this waiting time interval. The prophet instructs his students and listeners to wait patiently because the manifested goal *will surely come*. Note, HabakkuK did not say that something must or needs to be done by the petitioner.

Actually, a waiting period is also a cooling period. It gives you an opportunity to reconsider your wish or maybe even change your mind...

∽ひ◠

Fourth verse has two parts.

... his soul which is lifted up, is not upright in him.

This part refers to being in an emotionally excited state—the soul which is uplifted while envisioning the goal or intent. It is mentioned above that an emotionally excited state facilitates the manifestation of the desired result. If we are not upright—if we have mixed feelings or doubts (about the desired outcome)—it will cause a delay in manifestation and our "receiving" phase will tary—be tardy.

> KEY CONCEPT:
> Hold on to your faith—The Just shall live by his faith.

Belief. The second part of the fourth verse—*but the just shall live by his faith*—is key to successful manifestation. Wait, believe, have faith, and live as if the delivery of your goal is already an accomplished manifestation.

Holding the belief in your purpose is the requirement for its manifestation.

If you doubt your desired outcome, you stall the mechanism that assembles the components required to complete the manifestation of your objective.

HabakkuK said succinctly: "*The just shall live by his faith*". (Habakkuk 2:4).

In the original Hebrew it is said more succinctly—expressed in three words.[59]

For the universe to help you manifesting your project you have to *live in faith.* Faith in yourself and faith in your purpose.

St. Paul of Tarsus endorsed this rule of Habakkuk by quoting it twice in his epistles, (Romans 1:17 and Galatians 3:11). The unknown author of the epistle to the Hebrews (Hebrews 10:38), also quoted this same verse from Habakkuk (Habakkuk 2:4).

It all comes down to maintaining a continuing state of faith.

Faith is not a one-time act—faith is a way of life. Within the framework of this way of life—you get to manifest. Living *with* faith and living *in* faith cannot be overemphasized. Living in faith is forward looking. Living in faith is the theological touchstone of all great religions.

וְצַ·דִ··יק בֶּ·אֱמוּ·נָתוֹ יִ·חְ·יֶ·ה

ATTRACTING THE PRESIDENCY

Ronald Reagan attracted the presidency of the United States by using the LOA. His book title says it all: *"Reagan In His Own Hand: The Writings of Ronald Reagan That Reveal His Revolutionary Vision of America."*[60] This book narrates through eyewitnesses and original Reagan written files how between the years 1975–1979, Reagan *wrote* in his own hand, (no speech writer, and no ghost writer) a total of 670 radio speeches. In theses radio addresses he repeatedly communicated his *vision* for the United States of America.

Get this—the future president Ronald Reagan had a *vision* for himself and for America. He wrote his vision down and he communicated his vision in his speeches and addresses for four years, hundreds and hundreds of times. Then in 1979, he did something about it: he formed *a mastermind alliance* (known as the Reagan for President, Election Campaign Committee). Next he ran officially for the presidential primaries. He won his party's nomination. In 1980, he was elected as the 40th president of the United States. He won the elections against a sitting president. Reagan employed five Key Concepts of the LOA: having a vision, writing the vision down hundreds of times, proclaiming the vision to the public, recruiting a mastermind alliance and taking inspired actions.

THE LAW OF ATTRACTION MADE SIMPLE

Once a vision is conceived there is hardly a way back—the vision will manifest.

The master attractor in the book of Proverbs asserted it resolutely:

> *"For surely there is an end; and thine expectation shall not be cut off."* (Proverbs 23:18).

Note: There are no "ifs" and no "buts." Thine expectation is to be fulfilled.

Your vision is like an arrow shot out of a bow that is fulfilled—hitting its target—your expectation shall not be cut off. The expectation shall not

---

60   Ronald Reagan, Annelise Anderson, George P. Shultz and Martin Anderson. Reagan In His Own Hand: The Writings of Ronald Reagan That Reveal His Revolutionary Vision of America. Free Press. 2001.

be cut off—it cannot be cancelled. *Thine* (your) expectation is destined to manifest because your expectation is your thought and your thought thinks about itself and compounds itself growing in your mind. Gradually, as your awareness expands, you see evidence for your thought around you. When you see the evidence, you believe that your own thought is manifesting. As you believe your own eyes and ears *"thine expectation shall not be cut off."*

KEY CONCEPT:

The Law of Attraction is a gift that keeps on giving.

Chapter Seven

DONKEY TALES

For reasons unknown, the early authors and editors of the Bible assigned the *ass* a special role in visions, prophecy and intents that manifested great results.

The members of the committee of translators that King James appointed termed this hard working domestic animal—ass. Yes an ass. In our post-modern society an ass has diverse and politically-incorrect meanings. So I titled this chapter with the acceptable synonym *Donkey*. Yet in the Bible an *ass* is an ass.

The dictionary tells that an ass and a donkey are one and the same—a usual hard-working animal. A male ass is a jack—a jackass. A female ass is a jenny. Somehow we associate a jackass with stubbornness or stupidity. We are about to see in the following two Biblical stories that even a jackass has a compelling reason to behave as it does. Maybe for a divinely inspired reason...

THE PROPHET BLESSES BY WORDS

In the book of Numbers, chapters 22–24, we read a long story about the power of words to curse or to bless.

The background of the story involves the Children of Israel still following Moses on their trek to the Land of Canaan. God made a promise to Moses and the Israelites to be led into the Land of Canaan. We established in the first chapter of this book that Moses is the first grand master of the Law of Attraction.

In the course of their journey, the children of Israel pass near the kingdom of Moab. Balak, the King of Moab, distrusts the Israelites passing at his border. Balak takes action and retains a prophet named Balaam (*Bilaam* in Hebrew), whose job is to curse the Israelites. Balaam has a good reputation as an insightful prophet. Balak promises Balaam a fortune if he will curse the Israelites and get them away of the border of Moab. The prevailing reputation of Balaam is, *"Whom thou blessest is blessed, and he whom thou cursest is cursed."* The emissaries of Balak come to Balaam and he says that he wants to sleep on it a night. During his sleep God tells Balaam in a vision to **not curse** the children of Israel. Balak sends more honorable princes carrying greater rewards to beseech Balaam to come over and curse the Israelites. Balaam sleeps on it one more night and in the morning saddles his ass to go with the princes of Moab. God doesn't like it and sends an angel to block Balaam's path.

Except that Balaam doesn't recognize the angel. However his faithful ass recognizes the angel on her path and stops walking. Balaam loses his temper and gets angry at his loyal ass and beats it. The ass moves sideways and the leg of Balaam is crushed against a wall.

The ass sees something that even her master, the insightful prophet, does not recognize… The angel of God.

Balaam beats the ass again. The poor beaten ass asks Balaam:

"What have I done unto thee that thou hast smitten me these three times?" (Num. 22:28).

Balaam answers the ass:

"Because thou has mocked me: I would there were a sword in mine hand for now I would kill thee."

"And the ass said unto Balaam:

Am I not thine ass, upon which thou hast ridden ever since I was thine unto this day? Was I ever wont to do so unto thee?" (Num. 22:30).

This dialogue between a man and his ass has several meanings.

First, the ass is treated here as an intelligent human being that thinks for itself.

Second, the ass protests being treated with disrespect (like a jackass) by Balaam. Third, the ass gets emotional and reminds Balaam its loyal services for all the past years. The ass assumes in this episode a role of a household servant of many years and demands respect from Balaam its master. The ass acts and speaks like a human who possesses the capability of self-consciousness.

Third, the ass is a disguised intermediary between Balaam the prophet, and God's angel, who is also God's emissary.

This discussion became an eye-opener for Balaam as he finally recognized God's angel. Being a prophet of reputable integrity, Balaam speaks only what God tells him to say during his nightly vision. Balaam then tells three prophesies detailing God's covenant with Abraham (Numbers 23–24). The fourth prophecy names the nations that Israel would defeat (Numbers 24:15–25). This is bad news for Balak because one of the defeated nations is—Moab.

Eventually, all these prophesies materialized.

⊰⊱

Let us examine now the Key Concepts of the LOA that operate in this story of Balak and Balaam.

Balak, the King of Moab, appreciates the power of spoken word. He wants to use this power for his benefit. We see the belief in the power of the spoken words as a recurrent motive throughout the Bible. Words hold the power of self-fulfilling prophesy.

- Special people possess the power to pronounce and manifest. These are the people who are familiar with the LOA. Balaam was one such man.

- The special people who are familiar with the LOA get their inspiring ideas from their visions. The visions can occur during sleep as in a dream or they hear a voice talking to them. They may hear a donkey talking to them words of meaning.

- The prophets who are familiar with the LOA accept their cues from any *synchronous* or *serendipitous* event. The talking donkey could have easily been a whispering horse or a tweeting bird.

- People who are familiar with the powers of the LOA such as a prophet know that they can manifest goodness by expressing a blessing or can bring adversity by cursing. It is all a matter of belief in what one says or hears. And a belief is only a thought kept in the mind.

- A *belief* is a thought that is kept in the mind and draws to it associated thoughts that are the components required for the manifestation of the belief.

HE SEARCHED FOR LOST ASSES AND FOUND A MONARCHY

The next story involves lost asses.

The asses were the property of a man whose name was Kish and he was from the tribe of Benjamin. It is not known how many asses were lost. It could have been a herd of numerous asses—jacks and jennies and their nursing baby asses. Kish had a tall and imposing son whose name was Saul. So he sent his son and his servant to go and look for the lost asses and bring them back home. They went around the country and couldn't find the missing asses. Then Saul wanted to return home because his father, Kish, will get worried. However, the servant suggested that they will go ask the seer—a known prophet in the area—if he will assist locating the lost livestock.

Saul agreed to go see the man of God.

The great prophet was no one else other than Samuel, the son of Elkanah and Hannah. We met his parents in a previous chapter when they prayed to God for Hannah to get pregnant and their prayer was answered as promised by Eli the great priest of the time. Indeed, Elkanah and Hannah had a son—Samuel—who now plays the historical role of king-maker.

The people of Israel were not pleased with having a prophet overseeing them. They wanted a real king. Samuel the prophet listened to God. He was inspired by God to go along with the request of the people and anoint a king.

This king will be the first monarch of Israel.

Who would Samuel select and anoint to be king? What is the selection process?

Enter *serendipity* and *synchronicity*.

> *"And they went up into the city: and when they were come into the city, behold, Samuel came out against them, for to go up to the high place. Now the Lord has told Samuel in his ear a day before Saul came, saying, Tomorrow about this time I will send thee a man out of the land of Benjamin, and thou shalt anoint him to be captain over my people Israel... And when Samuel saw Saul, the Lord said unto him, Behold the man whom I spake to thee of! This same shall reign over my people."* (1 Samuel 9:14–17). The rest is history.

Yes, you may ask, but what about the lost asses?

Samuel the prophet had the answer to that small detail.

"When you art departed from me today, then thou shalt find two men by Rachel's sepulcher in the border of Benjamin at Zelzah; and they will say unto thee, The asses which thou wentest to seek are found..." (1 Samuel 10:2).

End of another donkey tale.

Two comments aimed at the "doubting Donald."

I can not add anything to the world class research and writings of Dr. Robert K. Merton of Columbia University, who received twenty honorary doctoral degrees from the top universities in the U.S. and around the world. His seminal works in support of the concepts of *self-fulfilling prophecy* and *serendipity* stands on their own merit.

Second, in my opinion, the asses in these biblical stories were a trigger that was needed to ignite the protagonist-prophets' inspiration.

The lesson is—that an ass has a mind of its own.

Chapter Eight

DAVID A MASTER
OF VISUALIZATION

Visualizations are an effective tool in doing the mental work in the process of attracting your very best in life—to you.

For attracting the best for yourself and your loved ones, rehearse frequently King David's master visualization—Psalm 23:

> *"The Lord is my shepherd; I shall not want.*
>
> *He maketh me to lie down in green pastures: he leadeth me beside the still waters.*
>
> *He restoreth my soul: he leadeth me in the path of righteousness for his name's sake.*
>
> *Yea, though I walk through the valley of the shadow of death, I will fear no evil: for thou art with me; thy rod and thy staff they comfort me.*
>
> *Thou preparest a table before me in the presence of mine enemies: thou anointest my head with oil; my cup runneth over.*
>
> *Surely goodness and mercy shall follow me all the days of my life: and I will dwell in the house of the Lord for ever."*

This visualization, my friend, is about two millennia old. Visualization is true and tried.

TOOL: VISUALIZATION

Visualization is a purposeful thought process that may or may not be related to a person's task at hand. The mind's eye or ear imagines pictures or sounds that are not consistent with the reality of the present moment.

It is estimated by neuro-psychiatrists that most people spend thirty percent of their waking hours spacing out, drifting, lost in their inner world of thoughts and pictures. We all "watch our mental videos." Some of our mental videos are positive and constructive. Other pictures are of negative nature. The "neuron default network" is an active brain structure that is responsible to imaginary visualizations.

A thought—any thought—good or bad, triggers and activates the LOA.

The poets and authors of the Bible recognized the important phenomenon of visualization. A good and beneficent visualization of the divine and its infinite goodness attracts heavenly circumstances to the life of the dreamer.

Chapter Nine

JOB TURNED ADVERSITY TO FORTUNE

O nce upon a time a man whose name was Job lived in the Land of Uz. Somewhere in the land of Arabia.

Job was perfect, upright and feared God.

He owned seven thousand sheep; three thousand camels (the Hummer vehicles of his time); five hundred oxen (like Caterpillar tractors); and five hundred she-donkeys. His household was the greatest of all the men in the East.

He had seven sons and three daughters. His seven sons and daughters feasted in their houses, everyone in his day.

After the feasts were over Job made offerings to God saying, *may be that my sons have sinned and cursed God in their heart*. Job feared God. See, Job harbored fears.

Then a day came and the fortunes of Job reversed.

A messenger came in to inform him that robbers from the Land of Sheba looted his livestock. Next walked in another runner telling that a fire burned his sheep. As if this was not enough more bad news broke, telling Job that the house where his sons and their families feasted was struck by a wild windy desert storm like a tornado, and his children and grandchildren died.

Yet Job did not blame God.

Job tore his clothing, shaved his head in mourning and said *"Naked came I out of my mother's womb and naked shall I returne thither."* (Job 1:21).

Next, Job's faith was tested by God when he was hit by *"skin sore boils from the sole of his foot unto his crown"*. (Job 2:7). Some sort of itchy chronic exematous dermatitis afflicted Job.

Yet Job did not blame God and did not curse God. Not even in his heart.

༚ஒ

Job had three friends who heard of his misfortunes and came to visit him *to mourn with him and to comfort him*. During the conversations that took place among those 4 wise men, Job confessed to his friends:

"For the thing which I greatly feared is come upon me, and that which I was afraid of is come unto me." (Job 3:25).

Job admitted that it was his own faulty negative thinking responsible for his misfortunes. He feared adversity and the LOA fulfilled his expectations and delivered to him the adversity he was so afraid of.

Job did not blame God.

༚ஒ

The famous great debate between Job and his three friends went on.

At some point in the discussion Eliphaz the Temanite (Yemenite) had an epiphany—he got the idea and said positively:

"Thou shalt also decree a thing and it shall be established unto thee: and the light shall shine upon thy ways." (Job 22:28).

Eliphaz agreed with Job's way of thinking and expressed his opinion in a positive attitude and declarative language.

The debate was long, hard and painful to the participants. Every speaker gained wisdom and insight. Even Job had a new insight.

Towards the end "*the Lord turned the captivity of Job, when **he prayed for his friends**; also the Lord gave Job twice as much as he had before... The lord blessed the latter end of Job more than his beginning ...*" (Job 42:10–12).

You see, something changed in Job's consciousness—a transformation of his way of thinking. Job abandoned the thoughts of fear—Job now prayed for his friends.

Note that when you pray an intercessory prayer on behalf of a friend, something happens in your own mind first. The change starts within our praying mind. Job abandoned thoughts of catastrophe and entered the phase of thoughts of *benestrophe*. Your prayer may or may not affect your friend but it affects you first and foremost.

So as Job prayed for his friends—his own health improved and he recovered from his skin condition. Next, the material fortunes manifested back in his life. Job was the first beneficiary from his intercessory prayer on behalf of his friends.

Lesson learned from Job: the process of healing, improvement and revitalization, be it health or wealth, begins in our own mind first.

Let us recall this psychological fact of life:

"*As a man thinketh in his heart so is he*". (Proverbs 23:7).

Earl Nightingale said it in modern English: *We become what we think about.*

Take a moment, sit back and watch your thoughts.

Do you decree a great fortune being established unto you? Or do you fear adversity? What do you think?

The conclusion is: When you decree your good fortunes "*the light shall shine upon your ways.*"

Chapter Ten

JESUS THE MASTER TEACHER

Jesus is referred to in the New Testament as the Master.[61]

During his ministry he was a master teacher[62] and healer, manifesting health, abundance and teaching ethics. The gospels document his repeated acts of healing and creating abundance to the multitudes.

Let us review the case of the healing in Nain, as the story unfolds in the gospel of Luke:

> *"And it came to pass the day after, that he went into a city called Nain;... when he came nigh to the gate of the city, behold, there was a dead man carried out, the only son of his mother, and she was a widow: and much people of the city was with her. And when the Lord saw her, he had compassion on her, and said unto her, Weep not. And he came and touched the bier: and they that bare him stood still. And he said, Young man, I say unto thee, Arise.*

---

61   Luke 17:13
62   Matthew 4:23

And he that was dead sat up, and began to speak. And he delivered him to his mother. And there came a fear on all and they glorified God..." (Luke 7:11–17).

The story relates that Jesus healed or brought from the dead a man into life by speaking to, and ordering him—Arise. We can speculate how "absolute dead" was the man. Was he just obtunded? Or in a coma? Maybe in catatonic paralysis? Hysterical? He could have been in any motionless state and was startled by the verbal order—Arise and by the entourage of Jesus. The point is that there was an act of decree—Arise, said by Jesus. The patient responded favorably to the order—he sat up, spoke, and was "delivered" back to his mother.

৵ৡ

We visited the village of Nain in Israel and the site of the healing before writing this chapter. Read our tour report in the Appendix to this book.

৵ৡ

ATTRACTING ABUNDANCE

The LOA[63] is promoted as a mindset to manifest abundance, prosperity, or amassing wealth. Abundance and wealth can take the form of essential supplies, provisions, property, money or lucrative objects.

Let us review the story of Jesus manifesting abundance.

The gospel of Mark illustrates Jesus' influence to attract and manifest food for multitudes of people: *He had taken the five loaves and the two fishes, he looked up to heaven, and blessed, and brake the loaves, and gave them to his disciples to set before them; and the two fishes divided he among them all... And they that did eat of the loaves were about five thousand men.* (Mark 6:41–44).

Note what Jesus did: *He looked up to heaven, and blessed...* This was an act of mental work that precedes or comes along with the manifestation of abundance. It may take the form of praying, meditating, or envisioning. The biblical narrative does not disclose the source of the manifested extra food. The

---

63   Note that LOA is also the acronym for Law of Abundance.

bread could have come through many channels: donations by local residents; the gathering could have been a picnic style potluck on the northwest shore of the Lake of Galilee. A petitioner-thinker who imposes restrictions or exclusions on the sources (channels) of supply and abundance diminishes the LOA potential for manifesting wealth.

Recall: once a thought is sparked in the mind, it starts to think about itself and generates collateral thoughts for the LOA to match desired abundance through heightened conscious awareness of universal opportunities of abundance.

Keep in mind the seventh **Key Concept**: The Law of attraction manifests through infinite springs of abundance.

A report of our visit to the beautiful site of the Church of Multiplication on the shore of the Lake of Galilee is included in the Appendix to this book.

Chapter Eleven

PAUL THE MASTER ATTRACTOR

Paul of Tarsus was a Master Attractor.

He still is, today, an exemplary awesome Master Attractor.

The proof is in the outcome of his missionary work—spreading successfully, Christianity from early on.

Paul experienced four visions. He was driven to action by his visions. He took guidance for action from his visions. Paul brought his message to people near and far. In order to bring the good news (*gospel*), he made countless personal appearances. He travelled inconveniently long distances for many weeks at a time. He traveled by any means of transportation available at his time. He journeyed on the back of camels, horses and sailed on open decks of sea-faring boats.

Paul was a writer. Paul wrote and sent letters (*epistles*) to publicize the gospel. Not all of his writings survived the decay of time.

Paul was a great communicator. He preached his vision and message in front of public audiences. He spoke to anyone who would listen to his message.

Today there are an estimated two billion people living on the face of the earth that consider themselves as Christians. The apostle Paul utilized the full powers of the LOA framework during his missionary life. He deployed every Key Concept of the LOA at one point or another.

Utilizing the Key Concepts of the LOA and the principles of the LOA, Paul was and still remains an unequaled publicity dynamo devoted to the cause of spreading the gospel. It is impossible to estimate the number of living men, women and children that he talked to, and preached to during his lifetime. There is no way to tell how many people were present in his audiences during his lifetime. He probably saw and talked face-to-face before several thousand unique persons during his lifetime ministry.

Further, Paul had his letters read and recited in public—in homes and in front of congregations (churches in Greek translation) in his absence—by emissaries. Two millennia later, his letters (*epistles*) are still read in public.

It is my intent in this chapter to show that Paul of Tarsus used all the Key Concepts of the Law of Attraction. His *modus operandi* was similar to the methods still employed today (21st century), by great communicators, artists, and politicians running for elections, evangelists, and salespeople. Contemporary technology provides videoconferencing, radio addresses, teleseminars and internet websites. Most marketers, politicians, preachers, singers, artists, and seminar promoters still go on the road and travel by air around the globe to present and promote—face to face—their cause, their message or sell their products. American politicians running for president start their primaries in Iowa going door to door and promoting their candidacy at voters' kitchen tables, known as "retail political campaigning."

So did Paul of Tarsus. He was an eager and willing retail, face-to-face evangelist if need be. So are many missionaries who still knock on doors to hand out gospel literature.

Paul marketed intangibles two millennia ago—the most difficult articles to sell. Nonetheless, he was successful in selling his ideas and message.

This chapter is not involved in the contents of Paul's theology.

This chapter is concerned with Paul's methods of winning friends and influencing people to accept the message of the gospel. If Paul was alive today in the age of Twitter he would have had over 2 billion "Followers." In Facebook parlance he would have scored over 2 billion "*Like*" clicks. Paul was the first to turn his followers into residents of *the global village*.[64] This notional *global village* is the globalism of the Christian faith today. This chapter also shows how often the messenger (St. Paul the apostle) becomes the message.[65], [66]

Paul's place of birth, according to the book of Acts, is in Tarsus, a city in Cilicia.[67] The teachings of the Catholic Church state that Paul was born in the year 8 CE.[68]

There are other scholarly opinions about Paul's early origins. Some historians think that Paul was born in 4 BCE to his Jewish parents and was raised in a village in northern Galilee called Jish in Arabic (or Gischala).[69] Today the place is called Gush Halav in northern Israel. His parents named him *Shaul* in Hebrew (Saul in Greek). His parents were taken captive by the Roman conquerors in 2 BCE and were exiled as slaves to the city of Tarsus in Cilicia (corner region between Turkey and Syria). At some point, the family was set free by their Roman masters and granted Roman citizenship.[70]

Paul was the beneficiary of wide education. He was fluent in Greek, Latin and Hebrew, or its closest dialect—Aramaic. At about age 19 he went to Jerusalem. Paul claims twice that he learned under the great Rabbi of his time—Rabban Gameliel. Paul was familiar with the Greek translation of the Hebrew Bible. In his early life, he was a Pharisee by his own testimony. There is no evidence that he was married or had children, something unusual for a Pharisee Jew.

---

64   The credit for this concept goes to Marshall McLuhan.

65   As Marshall McLuhan said: *The medium is the message.*

66   Roger Ailes: *You Are The Message.* Crown Business. 1989.

67   Acts 22:3. The author of the book of Acts quotes Paul speaking about himself in the temple in Jerusalem.

68   Pope Benedict XVI: *"Saint Paul"*. Ignatius Press. San Francisco. P. 14. 2009.

69   The Pauline scholar, Jerome Murphy-O'Connor, attributes this fact to St. Jerome. St. Jerome (*Eusebius Sophronius Hieronymus*, 347–420 AD), is considered a serious and talented linguist and a responsible historian by all Bible scholars. Jerome was a phenomenal polyglot by any standards. St. Jerome translated the Holy Bible from the original languages, Hebrew and Greek, into Latin (the Vulgate). As result, he was designated as a *doctor of the church*. Although he lived about 300 years after Paul his testimony is considered by many to be reliable.

70   Jerome Murphy-O'connor: *Paul His Story.* Oxford University Press. New York. 2004.

Later in his life, he went to learn firsthand from Peter whatever he could about the life and ministry of Jesus, since Peter was an eyewitness and pupil of Jesus, whereas Paul did not meet Jesus.

Paul was a prolific writer. He understood well the power of the written word. He is considered the author of thirteen of the epistles in the New Testament. Scholars believe, with little dispute, that he indeed wrote with his own hand seven out of the thirteen letters.[71], [72] The other six letters were possibly dictated by him to a scribe.

Paul was a public speaker who preached persuasive sermons and mounted his legal defense before Roman courts and on behalf of his companion-disciples.

Paul practiced healing—performing acts of attracting health and healing the sick. Those acts of healing were considered at the time, and remain today in many minds, impressive acts of manifesting "miracles."

Paul made full use of the Mastermind Alliance concept. Among his close associates and advisers were Luke, Barnabas, Silas and Timothy.

Paul was an empathic listener. He was empathic to other people's problems and their life challenges. He displayed the "I feel your pain" attitude. Does that sound familiar to you? As a result, he knew how and when to be of assistance to others. That gave him influential advantage in addition to being a tri-linguist, an author and a public speaker. All his talents synergistically enhanced his successful ministry to promoting the message of the resurrection, and human salvation through Jesus.

Stated in other words, Paul of Tarsus had a charismatic personality.

∽∂∾

The book of Acts chapter 9 introduces Paul and gives a recount of how Paul used Key Concepts of the Law of Attraction. Chapter 16 illustrates Paul's uses of the Key Concepts of the LOA.

The book of Galatians illustrates many of Paul's practices as narrated by him.

---

71   The seven letters that Paul wrote are Romans, Galatians, Corinthians (2 letters), Philippians, 1 Thessalonians and Philemon.
72   Albert Schweitzer: "The Mysticism of Paul the Apostle." Translated by William Montgomery. 1931. The John Hopkins University Press. Baltimore MD. 1998.

We shall examine Key Concept of the LOA and see how Paul deployed them effectively during the course of his successful ministry.

IT ALL STARTED WITH A VISION

Paul experienced four visions. According to the Book of Acts, Paul was inspired by each of his visions and was compelled to take action.

His first vision is the most famed one—his conversion on the road to Damascus.

> *"...And suddenly there shined round about him a light from heaven. And he fell to the earth, and heard a voice saying unto him..."* (Acts 9:3–4).
>
> *"...And the lord said unto him, Arise and go into the city, and it shall be told thee what thou must do. And the men which journeyed with him stood speechless, hearing a voice, but seeing no man."* (Acts 9:6–7).

Note that in his vision he was inspired to take action. However, the exact nature of the action was to be clarified later. Paul trusted his inspiration and followed the travel order in blind faith, not knowing what will happen to him next.[73]

A vision, a trance, or a dream can be an intense psychological transformative event to any person. The nature of the vision may be hallucinatory consisting of sights and sounds. Paul's psychological transformation did not end on the way to Damascus circa 35 CE. According to his own written testimony Paul continued to experience psychological changes. His evolving transformation was now inspired by God. *"But when it pleased God, who separated me from my mother's womb, and called me by his grace, To reveal his son in me, that I might preach him among the heathen, immediately I conferred not with flesh and blood: Neither went I to Jerusalem to them which were apostles before me; but I went into*

---

73   The word *blind* is more than a pun in this situation. Paul was actually double blinded.

Arabia, and returned again unto Damascus. Then After three years I went up to Jerusalem to see Peter..." (Gal. 1:15–18).

After his conversion Paul continued to live three years in personal isolation in the desert of Arabia—the region of the Nabataean town of Petra, west of the city of Maan and north of Aqaba, Jordan. He was not the first biblical visionary who chose personal isolation in the desert and returned back to structured society with a claim of having received a divine message.

∾⟨ิ∾

After the famed revelatory episode, on the way to Damascus, Paul had subsequently three additional vision experiences.

Second vision. In Troas, we find that Paul was unsure how to proceed in his missionary journey. After some hesitation, *"...a **vision** appeared to Paul in the night; There stood a man of Macedonia and prayed him, saying, Come over into Macedonia, and help us."* (Acts, 16:7–9). Once he experienced the vision he regained his assuredness and proceeded to act with notable success.

Third vision. In Corinth, Paul encountered opposition to his teachings. *"Then spake the Lord to Paul in the night by a **vision**, Be not afraid but speak, and hold not thy peace: For I am with thee, and no man shall set on thee to hurt thee: for I have much people in this city."* (Acts 18:9–10).

Fourth vision. In Jerusalem, Paul spoke at the temple and his preaching created controversial tumult among the throngs of resisting worshipers. Soldiers had to carry him to the castle where he was detained for his own safety and for the public order. Paul requested to be heard by the council of priests, and his defense speech created further dissention among the restive audience. *"And the night following the Lord stood by him, and said, Be of good cheer, Paul: for as thou hast testified of me in Jerusalem, so must thou bear witness also at Rome."* (Acts 23:11). Paul needed all the courage he could muster for the demanding task that lay ahead of him. Paul followed each of his visions with inspired action.

∾⟨ิ∾

PAUL BENEFITS FROM SYNCHRONICITY

Synchronicity is an enabling mechanism of the Key Concepts of the LOA.

It is the experience of two (or more) events that are occurring together in a manner that is meaningful to the observers of the event.

The synchronous events cannot be explained as a cause and effect. Only persons with a mindset towards attaining a clear intent or a goal will have the capability of capturing the synchronicity of the events. That happens because the RAS of the tuned-in minds are awake, alert and on the lookout for the desired and expected circumstance.

Paul benefited from events of *synchronicity.*

As he embarked on the road entering Damascus, complying with the vision he experienced, he met his appointed supporter—Ananias.

While Paul gets closer to Damascus, a drama occurs within the city limits: another man (Ananias), experiences an independent vision.

> *"...and there was a certain disciple at Damascus, named Ananias; and to him said the Lord in a vision, Ananias. And he said, Behold, I am here Lord. And the lord said unto him, Arise, and go to the street which is called Straight , and enquire in the house of Judas for one called Saul of Tarsus: for behold, he prayeth, and hath seen in a vision a man named Ananias coming in, and putting his hand on him, that he might receive his sight."* (Acts 9:10–12).

However, Ananias had some reservations:

> *"Lord, I have heard by many of this man, how much evil he hath done to thy saints at Jerusalem:"* (Acts 9:13). Nonetheless, his reservations are overruled: *"But the Lord said unto him, Go thy way: for he is a chosen vessel unto me, to bear my name before the Gentiles, and kings, and the children of Israel."* (Acts 9:15).

Thus, while Paul was following his vision, another man—Ananias—had experienced *synchronously* an independent vision that directed him to assist Paul.

This synchronous episode—of two visions compelled two different persons to take inspired actions towards manifesting a mutual objective is an attractor event.

✧❧

LIFE SAVING SYNCHRONICITY

While on their missionary journey, Paul and Silas stayed in Philippi, where Paul preached his gospel. The local authorities did not approve of the new customs that Paul taught and placed him and Silas in jail. "*And at midnight Paul and Silas prayed, and sang praises unto God: … And suddenly there was a great earthquake, so that the foundations of the prison were shaken: and immediately all the doors were opened, and everyone's bands were loosed.*" (Acts 16:25–26).

Here again Paul is the beneficiary of *synchronous* events and he gets released from prison during an earthquake (which is not a rare event in Macedonia). Moreover his belief system gets the credit for the "miraculous" release from captivity and turned his jailors into converts. We now know that there is no *coinky-dink* in life. Synchronicity is available to every person who expects it with an open mind.

✧❧

Key Concepts—from the framework of the LOA that took place in Acts, chapters 9 and 16 are:

- Two men who each experienced a *vision.*
- Two men who each took *inspired action* in their respective time and place, following a vision.
- *Synchronicity* connected the two men who each had a vision.
- The LOA *matched* two men in need with solutions using its own sources of supply.
- The LOA has unforeseen *infinite* channels of supply to meet any person's need.
- The LOA is *inclusive*—it does not discriminate among persons.

Paul Used Mastermind Alliances

In the course of these events, Paul and Ananias formed a *mastermind alliance*.

Paul's mastermind circle of allies grew larger when he was joined later by Barnabas, Luke, Silas and Timothy.

Writing Down The Vision And The Objectives

History tells us that Paul excelled as a great author and writer.

He wrote thirteen letters to the Christian communities in the Roman-Hellenic world. Those are known as his thirteen epistles. He explained to his readers, followers and listeners his views on theology, ethics, life and… life after death. Hence,

Paul repeatedly committed his visions and objectives in writing.

The LOA prefers and responds better to written goals and objectives.

The neuro-motor activity of writing etches onto the mind (brain's organsystem) the desired objective. Written goals and objectives launch the LOA into action. Subsequently, manifestation takes place.

Paul probably wrote many more epistles to the communities where he visited and preached the gospel. Not all his written letters survived down the path of history. However what came down to us[74] shows that in some cases he wrote more than one letter to the community as is the case with Corinthians 1 & 2 and Colossians 1 & 2. The contents of his epistles addressed a wide variety of life issues.

The Roman Catholic pontiffs write and publish encyclical rulings on various matters that are before the church as did St. Paul of Tarsus.

Pundits and celebrity politicians publish their opinions on their websites. So do contemporary bloggers and periodic newsletter publishers. Isn't it the same practice as Paul did?

President Obama recruited over 19 million fans (and potential voters) to his Facebook fan-page in the 2008 election year and communicated

---

74 Scholars estimate that to date, about 5,400 hand-written early manuscripts of the New Testament, partial or complete, are preserved in various libraries around the world.

with them. In the 2012 election season he attracted over 30 million fans ("Likes"). He solicits campaign funds, expresses his political views on many issues of the day, and still tries to inspire hope and change. Strategically, politicians, rulers and public relations people operate much the same today as the church preachers did 1,950 years ago. The only difference is the technological advances that amplified the tactics of outreach to the public.

Paul Demonstrated Unconditional Faith

Paul quoted Habakkuk's article of faith in two separate epistles.[75]

The just shall live by his faith.[76]

It is the intention of this book to avoid matters of theology. Nonetheless, to set the LOA into action a measure of faith is required. It is the same basic faith and belief that you'll wake up tomorrow morning and the sun shall also rise.

Paul had an unshakable belief in his message that became the foundation of his optimism. Optimism is way more conducive for manifestation and co-creation than a hopeless outlook on life.

Paul The Co-Creator

The ultimate outcome of Paul's missionary work was to launch Christendom, with over two billion followers.

Paul of Tarsus was a co-creator.

In his efforts he co-created a religious movement, a social movement, a system of ethics and a sovereign State. As a result he changed reality and contributed together with others to the Western civilization as we know it.

---

75 Romans 1:17 and Galatians 3:11
76 Habakkuk 2:4. See also chapter 6.

Paul The Communicator

In order to influence you have to communicate.

Paul of Tarsus was a phenomenal communicator.

He communicated face to face orally. He communicated in writing. And he communicated through emissaries and trusted followers who read his epistles in front of live audiences in churches. His epistles are still read today.

Paul employed every one of the ten Key Concepts listed as the framework components of the LOA discussed in earlier chapters of this book.

The Framework Of Paul's Ministry

As a Master Attractor, Paul displayed several traits that rendered him charismatic to other people with whom he came in contact.

Paul was an *empathic listener*.

He acknowledged the contents, the difficulties and the beliefs of his audience. Paul did not belittle nor avoided the difficult contents and interests that his listeners presented to him.

Paul respected the needs of his audience.

He saw their needs—the spiritual and physical needs and attempted to meet their needs. He responded to his audience. We know that individuals who display the quality of empathy are often perceived as "charismatic." Charismatic as in being an attractive and magnetic person.

Paul was also revered by his followers for another reason. He performed what was referred to as miracles ("*signs and wonders*"). The book of Acts narrates at least six episodes where Paul directly cured persons he met during his ministry.[77] Paul was associated with Luke and referred to Luke as his "*beloved physician.*" I assume that the two apostles (healers) shared their medical knowledge and put it to practical use whenever the opportunity occurred. In return they garnered respect and admiration from their beneficiaries and the witnesses to the healing episodes. A surefooted way to win friends and influence people.

Paul's ability to heal sick people and manifest health contributed to his credibility and persuasive persona.

---

77   Acts 14:3; Acts 14:8-18; Acts 19:11-12; Acts 20:7-12; Acts 28:7-8; Acts 28:9.

The third element in Paul's attractive personality is the keen perception when his followers needed food or material support.[78] When he recognized that relief was needed—he took action to collect and provide the required necessities.

Thus Paul was involved, at least twice, in famine relief and financial support to the community in Jerusalem. Paul leveraged his influence—by directing a methodical fundraising on the first day of the week. Then the collections were brought unto Jerusalem.[79]

There was famine during the reign of Claudius Caesar (46–49 CE). The disciples in Antioch "...*every man according to his ability, determined to send relief unto the brethren which dwelt in Judaea: Which also they did, and sent it to the elders by the hands of Barnabas and Saul.*" (Acts 11:29–30).

The second relief effort occurred in 57 CE when Paul arrived for his last visit to Jerusalem with a collection of money for the local congregation.[80] It was a humanitarian mission. No wonder he attracted followers—Paul delivered.

Paul of Tarsus was the first to organize and integrate humanitarian projects along with preaching of the gospel. The systematic missionary and humanitarian programs were never abandoned in the course of history of the Christian church. The church continues to the present day to maintain the traditional framework of missionary, education and welfare programs.

---

78 "*Only they would that we should remember the poor; the same which I also was forward to do.*" (Gal. 2:10).
79 1 Cor. 16:1-3
80 Acts 24:17 and Gal. 2:10.

PART THREE

MODERN DAY
MASTER ATTRACTORS

WHO IS A
MASTER ATTRACTOR?

Here is an answer to the basic question:

Who is a Master Attractor?

A Master Attractor is a person who manifests any two of the following four characteristics.

- A Master Attractor is a person who draws a large number of fans, admirers, or devotees.
- A Master Attractor creates new value in the domains of science, technologies, or enhances people's health and welfare.
- A Master Attractor is perceived as a spiritual or inspirational source by society.
- A master Attractor manifests material abundance by ethical means.

Master Attractors are dynamic persons. Master Attractors think differently. Great attractors are change agents. They know how to act in alignment with the Law of Attraction. Folks sense a great attractor when they see or hear one. Once a name of a person who may be a Master Attractor comes up, the audience identifies intuitively this personality as a great attractor. Folks do not need definitions and criteria to recognize a Master Attractor.

In this era of burgeoning social media you get a literal measure of the number of fans and devotees attracted to a personality. Only select few celebrities in the field of entertainment are inspirational. The market place often recognizes a Master Attractor.

The fourth criterion has inherent softness. The value of any asset is a matter of subjective perceptions. Material abundance is difficult to appraise and has no absolute standard. Ask any realtor about the value of a property or watch how inflation wipes out the value of equities.

Chapter Twelve

ALBERT SCHWEITZER

lbert Schweitzer demonstrated to us that *every useful life is a ministry.* He was a Master Attractor and co-creator. To create his life-long ministry he had to be a master attractor.

Albert Schweitzer was born on January 14, 1875. He was a prodigy from youth. By age thirty he earned doctoral degrees in the areas of Theology, Philosophy, Musicology and Medicine.

Schweitzer was a son of a protestant pastor in Alsace on the border between Germany and France. After graduation from high school his higher education continued simultaneously in theology, philosophy and music. He studied at the University of Strasbourg (1893–1898). He first became an ordained pastor and later earned his higher degree in theology. He was awarded a PhD degree in philosophy for his work titled *The Religious Philosophy of Kant* (1899). During summer breaks he studied music and practiced playing the organ in Paris with a great organ player of the time (Charles-Marie Widor) and wrote his first book on the renowned French musicologist Eugene Munch.

After realizing his graduate collegiate achievements, Schweitzer continued to study and wrote on theological subjects. His writings involved the history, teachings and meanings of the works of Jesus and Paul of Tarsus. Later he wrote also on the Buddhist and Hindu religions. As an organ player he gave public concerts and became a recognized interpreter of *J.S. Bach* musical works for organ in Europe. He wrote a major academic text on J.S. Bach and a book on the art of building church organs that is relevant to the present day.

As a man of a towering intellect, Schweitzer was inspired to live the higher life of service to humanity. As early as age twenty-one he decided to devote his life to service of humanity beginning at age thirty. At age twenty-nine Schweitzer decided to study medicine in order to serve later as a missionary physician in Equatorial Africa. He found that in Gabon was a lack of medical care and decided to settle there as a missionary physician. For that purpose he went to medical school to get the required medical education.

In the context of the Key Concepts of the Law of Attraction, Schweitzer had a *vision* for himself and he started to take *action* in order to manifest his vision.

According to Dr. Schweitzer:

> *"Thought is the strongest thing we have. Work is done by true and profound thought. That is the real force."*[81]

Albert Schweitzer studied medicine at the University of Strasbourg during the years 1905–1912. He then married his wife who was a nurse. In 1913 he graduated with an MD degree.

The next step in bringing his vision to life was to gather the funding for the medical mission station. With his wife, friends and other supporters Dr. Schweitzer embarked on lecture tours and concerts to raise funds for the envisioned medical facility that he will launch in Lambarene, Gabon. With friends' assistance, the funds were raised and the medical supplies to provide the care were purchased and packaged in crates. In 1913 he departed with his wife on board a ship to West Africa. Using the medical supplies and medicines

---

81   Erica Anderson: The Schweitzer Album. New York, Harper & Row Publishers. 1965. Inside back dustcover flap. Seems that Schweitzer knew that "thoughts become things."

he launched the clinic and built a hospital and a medical leper colony in Lambarene on the banks of the Ogowe River.

Dr. Schweitzer was a prolific writer and continued his *writing* practice in the jungle. His work in tropical Africa is documented in pocket diaries that he maintained and books he wrote and later would send for publication in Europe. Dr. Schweitzer designed and sketched in his handwriting the missionary medical station, the buildings and their dimensions. Then he manifested it with the help of volunteers and natives' assistance.

"Thought must be active. It must affect something."[82]

Since 1950, the ongoing work and the expansion of the medical facility in Lambarene as well as his public appearances in Europe, were systematically photographed and preserved on film.[83] Dr. Schweitzer was well aware of the relevance and importance of communication and public relations to raising funds for the clinic's operations and the capital improvements necessary for continuing modernization of the medical technology. He did all of that.

Under the inspiration of the scenic life in Africa, Dr. Schweitzer conceived and wrote his major original philosophical concept known as *Reverence for Life*. He subsequently wrote his major philosophical treatise *The Philosophy of Civilization* (1923). He was honored by numerous universities. In 1952 he was awarded the Nobel Peace Prize. Dozens of institutions—schools, hospitals, colleges and societies are now named after him. Governments printed honorary postal stamps with his profile. His fame and moral authority in Europe, U.K. and America grew and he was surrounded by a growing body of followers, volunteers and fans.

Using his income from books sales, royalties from music recordings, live concerts and lectures' proceeds, he funded for the following 40 years, the medical facility in Lambarene.

Alongside the medical and humanitarian mission, Dr. Schweitzer preached the gospel in Lambarene, Gabon. The duality of his missions bears

---

82 Erica Anderson: The Schweitzer Album. New York, Harper & Row Publishers. 1965. Page 161.
83 Ibid.

resemblance to the tradition set by Paul of Tarsus—preaching the gospel and healing the sick.

Dr. Albert Schweitzer demonstrated in his life-work and legacy how to harness the Key Concepts of the Law of Attraction.

- Albert Schweitzer had a vision. He took *action to manifest his vision*—he worked on it throughout his life and his vision grew larger than life.
- Dr. Albert Schweitzer committed *his vision in writing*. He published over two dozen books (in English translation) and recorded music.
- Schweitzer was a great communicator as a *public speaker*.
- Dr. Schweitzer developed through his ever growing circle of friends and supporters—*a mastermind alliance*. His friends and followers enabled him to raise funds in Europe and the U.S. to sustain the medical facility in Africa.
- His humanistic approach of *reverence for life*—regardless of ethnic and national differences—is an *inclusive principle*. His missionary medical facility treated very sick folks with tropical diseases without discrimination. His practice of *inclusivity* attracted people, volunteers and materiel in support of the now world-famed initiative.

Dr. Schweitzer passed away in on September 4, 1965, at age 90 years.

Chapter Thirteen

BILLY GRAHAM

The Reverend Billy Graham is the greatest master attractor of our lifetime.

In our era of burgeoning social media platforms and expanding communication services, attraction clout is a measurable metric. U.S presidents are leading attractors while they run for election or serve in office. Presidents and high office elected officials have a dual attraction objective: making their persona appear charismatic and presenting their political agenda attractively to the voters. However, a president's attraction clout may be transient and often self-limited to their term of service in office. While in office, they may lose their clout with the electorate and retire after serving only one term in office. Entertainers can be attractors while they are in vogue. Their popularity with the public is ephemeral. Once they lose their creative talents or voice they go out of style and lose their attraction clout.

The Reverend Billy Graham is a solid master attractor since his great historic rally in the fall of 1949 in Los Angeles. He commands the public's respect, attention, and admiration sixty-three years later. Billy Graham is known as the national pastor. He was awarded the Congressional Gold Medal and numerous other honors.

In writing this chapter I relied on Billy Graham's autobiography, "*Just As I Am*" [84] and the scholarly text "*The Leadership Secrets of Billy Graham.*"[85]

LANDMARK EVENTS IN THE LIFE OF BILLY GRAHAM

Billy Franklin Graham was born on a dairy farm near Charlotte NC, in 1918. At age sixteen he attended a revival meeting and was first time converted. He next attended Bob Jones College in 1936 and then transferred to the Florida Bible Institute. He later transferred to Wheaton College in Wheaton, Illinois and graduated in 1943 with a degree in anthropology. While in Wheaton College he had a religious experience and decided to accept the Bible as the infallible word of God. After graduation he married his wife Ruth who was his classmate. They had together five children. Ruth Bell Graham passed away in 2007.

In 1943 Billy Graham became an ordained pastor in nearby Western Springs, Illinois. When in 1944 a religious radio program in Chicago was about to go off the airwaves, Graham, with the financial support of his church members, took on the time slot and launched a radio ministry. He recruited George Beverly Shea as the director of the radio ministry. Later, George Beverly Shea became a major Team Member of the Billy Graham Evangelical Association (BGEA).

Billy Graham took on a career of a traveling evangelist in the 1940s with the Youth for Christ ministry. He made numerous public appearances in cities across the U.S. and in Europe in 1946. This period was a preparation experience for him.

Between 1947 and 1949 he conducted his first revival crusades. The 1949 revival event under tents in a parking lot in Los Angeles was the period when Graham turned into a prominent national figure.

Serendipitous public promotion from the printed press assisted the 1949 public crusade in Los Angeles. William Randolph Hearst directed his

---

84   Billy Graham: *Just As I Am: The Autobiography of Billy Graham*. HarperCollins, 1999.
85   Harold Myra & Marshall Shelley: *The Leadership Secretes of Billy Graham*. Zondervan 2005.

newspaper chain to promote Billy Graham's crusade in Los Angeles. Billy Graham describes what he saw for the first time as the crusade place was crawling with reporters and photographers, "I asked one of the journalists what was happening. *You have been kissed by William Randolph Hearst,* he responded." This phenomenon repeated itself in other big cities in the U.S. The legend has it that Mr. Hearst attended the public crusade incognito and was impressed by Billy Graham and decided to promote his ministry.

Time magazine joined the print media acclaim of Billy Graham in November of 1949. *Time* and *Life* magazines carried the story. Henry Luce, the owner of the magazines, was a son of Christian missionaries in China. In reality Henry Luce also acted on the favorable advice of Bernard Baruch who was then adviser to U.S presidents. Later, in 1954, *Time* magazine placed the portrait of Billy Graham on the front cover. The front cover exposure amplified the evangelical mission of Billy Graham and his worldwide reputation.

Billy Graham was invited for a visit with Archbishop Richard Cushing of Boston in 1964. This visit provided a helpful Catholic recognition to the BGEA ministry.

≪೧ஒ≫

As the ministries expanded their outreach, the business needs required a formal incorporation into a non-profit organization. The statement of incorporation expressed the mission and purpose in a simple sentence: *"To spread and propagate the gospel of Jesus Christ by any and all means."*

This clear mission statement is crucial to understanding the focus and direction of the activities of BGEA from its inception to present. In simple terms, all present and future opportunities to preach the gospel were hence attracted to manifest this goal.

≪೧ஒ≫

In the 1950s the challenge of ethnic segregation among audiences during evangelical campaigns had to be resolved. The campaign meetings were mixed, however ropes separated between black and white attendees. At one point Billy Graham removed the ropes before a rally in Jackson Mississippi (1952). Thus the campaign became desegregated. Billy Graham acted ahead of the Supreme Court decision of 1954 by two years, in implementing desegregation at his campaigns. He resisted pressure and criticism by segregationists. Better yet, he actively supported the work of Martin Luther King Jr.

Billy Graham implemented desegregation based on his own evangelical convictions and beliefs. However, Graham operated in alignment with the LOA. As mentioned in earlier chapters, the LOA is non-discriminatory. Its benefits are available to every human being.

Recall the earlier quote—*there is no exclusion in an attraction based universe. There is only inclusion.* Preaching the gospel and attracting new believers is inconsistent with segregation (exclusion). The success of the crusades was based on the correct inviting call: "Come as you are." Any kind of segregation was contrary to this philosophy and belief.

∾∾

In his memoir Billy Graham tells the history of his gradual evangelistic breakthrough into the atheist Soviet Union that eventually resulted in three crusades in later years. This dramatic struggle spanned over twenty-five years and demonstrates how Billy Graham worked in alignment with the Key Concepts of the LOA. Billy Graham was no fan of communism. He criticized the communist system for denying freedom of worship to all religions. Whatever few churches were left in the Soviet Union were tightly controlled by the communist regime.

According to his memoir the Soviet Union crusade started with a *dream* and a *prayer*.

In 1959 Billy Graham and Grady Wilson were granted tourist visas to visit Moscow. Among other sites they visited the large Lenin Stadium. There he tells, *"As we sat gazing out over its vast expanse, I bowed my head and prayed that someday God would open the door for us to preach the Gospel in Moscow…"*

Note that in order to manifest there was first a thought expressed in the form of prayer. In 1982, twenty-three years later, after lengthy diplomatic and media wrangling he was invited to speak in Moscow in the course of a communist, state- sponsored international religious conference. The negotiated arrangements included permission for Reverend Graham to preach in two Moscow churches: The Baptist Church and the Russian Orthodox Church. Graham was also hosted by a member of the Soviet Politburo and given a tour in the Kremlin.

The low-key 1982 sermons in Moscow were a small step towards manifesting his original dream and prayer from 1959.

In 1984 the Soviets concluded that it was to their advantage to allow Billy Graham to conduct a preaching mission in four of their major cities. This was a formal evangelical preaching tour.

In 1988 Billy Graham had another visit to the Soviet Union following a meeting with the communist party secretary general, Mikhail Gorbachev, who visited Washington a year earlier. Graham was given everywhere official reception. He spoke in front of an audience of 15,000 people in the Cathedral of Kiev. The Red Army provided a logistic support unit to the cathedral in order to ensure adequate electric power for the event. ("Let there be light" and let the television satellites broadcast world-wide). This kind of preaching environment was in line with Graham's expectations.

In 1991 Billy Graham returned to Moscow to open a BGEA sponsored evangelism training conference. In the following year, during another Moscow Revival, 155,000 people attended the Olympic Stadium. Billy Graham's dream manifested into reality.

Dreams have their path and timeline of manifesting into reality. As the saying goes, be careful what you ask in your prayers because you may get it and then some more.

∽◈∾

By the 1990s Billy Graham had evangelistic crusades in many countries which were difficult to penetrate like North Korea and China.

One more notable accomplishment: the closing of the Crusade in Seoul, South Korea in 1973 was attended by *one million people.*

∽◈∾

KEY CONCEPTS OF THE LOA USED BY BILLY GRAHAM

Based on the narrative above we can identify Key Concepts of the LOA in Billy Graham's ministries and life-time achievements.

The Mission

Billy Graham has a focused view of his mission. Quoting his words:

> *"God called me to preach and I do not intend to do anything else as long as I live."*

He stated his mission elsewhere succinctly: *"I just want to lobby for God."*

Billy Graham would not be distracted from his mission. He declined invitations to act in movies and film productions. Billy Graham declined a political career offered to him by President Lyndon Johnson.

A Mastermind Alliance—The Team

Billy Graham attracted around him an inner circle of Team Members that served as a mastermind alliance for many years to come, including service as executive board members of the BGEA. Notable Team Members from inception include Cliff Barrows, Grady Wilson and George Beverly Shea. During different periods there were other fellow evangelists on The Team.

Billy Graham chaired the board of BGEA. He characterized the board's work and unique nature of contributions by using the biblical verse *"in the multitude of counselors there is wisdom."*

Services—The BGEA Ministries

BGEA ministries are educational services for outreach to the public.

- *Hour of Decision*, a weekly radio program, broadcast around the world for more than 50 years.

- *Mission television* broadcast specials were regularly broadcast in prime time in most media markets in the U.S. and Canada.
- A syndicated newspaper column, *My Answer*, carried by newspapers across the United States.
- *Decision* magazine, the official publication of the BGEA.
- *Christianity Today* magazine, founded in 1956.
- *Passageway.org*, a website for a children's program.
- *World Wide Pictures* produced and distributed more than 130 films.
- Billy Graham is a prolific author. He wrote and published at least 29 books.

Communication - The Power of Public Speaking

Billy Graham is a charismatic public speaker.

His appearances in the U.S. began in 1945 as part of his work for Youth for Christ ministry. Billy Graham liked to visit and speak before student audiences in colleges and universities. In 1945, Billy Graham visited 47 states, logged 135,000 frequent flyer miles and was designated by United Airlines as its top civilian passenger.

BGEA records state that Billy Graham preached the gospel in person more than any other person in history. He preached in person to live audiences estimated at 185 million people on every continent. His lifetime audience via radio, television and webcasts is estimated at over 2.2 billion.

Continuous Innovation

Continuous innovation is a consistent characteristic of Billy Graham's organization. *"Geared to the times, anchored to the Rock,"* was the motto of YFC. Since the mid-forties the various modalities of communications were continuously adapted to the changing technology of the time. While the mission remained the same, communicating the gospel employed new progressive and far reaching technologies. Billy Graham stated, *"We used every modern means to catch attention."*

By 1954 Billy Graham broadcast the evangelistic program—*The Hour of Decision* on both ABC and NBC radio networks.

In 1995 Billy Graham stood on a pulpit in Puerto Rico and delivered his sermon via 30 transmission satellites to 185 countries. It is estimated that *one billion people* heard his message on that occasion.

Social Media platforms were adopted as they were introduced on the Internet. Social media evangelism is the channel of communication with mainly younger folks. As this line is written the combined Billy Graham and BGEA pages on Facebook have over one million "Likes." BGEA has presence on Google+.

The approach of Billy Graham is straight forward:

"I have the greatest product in the world. Why shouldn't it be promoted as well as soap?"

Public Relations
Billy Graham recognized the significance of professional public relations to amplify his preaching the gospel.

A. Larry Ross Communications has for many years been the full time public relations service for BGEA.

Russ Busby is the official photographer for BGEA. He took thousands of photos documenting Billy Graham's ministry.

Serendipitous Encounters
Early in his ministry Billy Graham attracted the attention (*serendipitously*) of influential American public figures who were impressed by his work and propelled his ministry to new heights.

- William Randolph Hearst
- Henry Luce
- Cardinal Richard Cushing

• Billy Graham met with the last 12 United States presidents serving in office, beginning with President Harry Truman.

Serendipity is listed three times in the book, *The Leadership Secrets of Billy Graham* by Myra and Shelley. Serendipity is more than a chance coincidence. Serendipity requires preparation work as we have seen in earlier chapters of this book. Only the prepared are ready for serendipitous encounters. The authors claim that Billy Graham benefitted from serendipity because of "thousands and thousands of seeds sowed" by him beforehand.

Inclusiveness – the Essence of Attraction

Billy Graham accepted all *people as they are* if they want to hear the message of the gospel. His stated principle is avoidance of doing anything that will shut the door to the gospel before any person.

His autobiography is titled *"Just As I Am."*

Indeed, the Key Concepts of the LOA are available equally to every human being. There is no exclusion in an attraction based universe.

George Beverly Shea

The concepts of inclusiveness and the practice of a mastermind alliance spawned collateral careers under the auspices of BGEA.

George Beverly Shea is a Master Attractor who blossomed within that flower bed.

Shea is one of the original Team Members of BGEA from its early days and a member of Billy Graham's mastermind alliance. Born in 1909, Shea is a gospel singer whose creativity and art flowered while singing solos during the crusades. Shea sang at the second Billy Graham crusade in the Old Armory in Charlotte, NC (1947).

George Beverly Shea wrote five hundred songs. He is a twice Grammy Awards winner.

His lifetime live audience is estimated at 220 million people. He is cited in *Guinness Book of Records* as the singer who sang in person in front of the most people ever.

Shea authored four books and received two honorary doctoral degrees.

His authorized biography, *George Beverly Shea: Tell Me the Story*, by Paul Davis was published in 2009. This biography is a collectors' item.

Above all, Bev Shea celebrated his 103 birthday.

What is the secret of George Beverly Shea who *knows how to attract people and attract health and longevity*?

I found partial answers to this question. Bev Shea left a hand-scribbled clue at the bottom end of his appreciation note to Paul Davis who wrote his authorized biography. There is his signature and below it he wrote in hard to decipher the letters *Psalms 28:7*. It took us a while to figure it out. When my friend said, *"Its Psalms,"* I turned to my Bible and opened it on Psalms 28:7 to read:

> *"The Lord is my strength and my shield;*
> *My heart trusted in him, and I am helped:*
> *Therefore my heart greatly rejoiceth;*
> *And with my song will I praise him."*

Anyone who rejoices with songs of praise in his heart cannot get sick. Songs of praise in your heart keep your blood pressure controlled and immune system boosted.

It is a common observation that creative artists such as painters, poets, writers and singers are blessed with a longer life span. Healthy genes are definitely a contributive factor to longevity. But a joyous heart full of praise is better protected from ailment and the body is more resistant to development of cancer.

Time magazine published in 2009 a special issue dedicated to *Mind & Body* with emphasis on faith, healing and longevity. Among the studies cited in the center article is one from the University of Michigan showing that folks who never attend religious services have twice the risk of dying over the next eight years as people who attend public religious services once a week. Another study from University of Pittsburgh Medical Center confirms that church attendance accounts for two to three additional years of life. Among other findings in this study—exercise accounts for three to five extra years of life. The interpretation given is that people who partake in a religious community are more likely to rely on one another for friendship, support, ride-sharing for errands and benefit from the social safety net the fellowship provides.

We are far from completely understanding how to attract health and longevity. Yet, I am more profoundly impressed by Bev Shea's demonstrated ability to attract health and longevity than by his world record of on-stage live performances. It was my privilege to publish a blog post celebrating his 103 birthday.[86]

---

86 http://themasterattractor.blogspot.com/2012/02/george-beverly-shea.html

Chapter Fourteen

ROGER BANNISTER

Life must be lived forwards even if sometimes it only makes sense as we look back.

—Sir Roger Bannister

This book highlights the use of the LOA mainly by biblical sages and heroes of yore. However, present day heroes of personal development and cutting edge technology use the LOA framework right now, in our lifetime. Take, for example, Steve Jobs who revolutionized computer technology, telecommunications, and entertainment industries. During his short career he acted as a Master Attractor to ideas, inventions, customers, fans and he touched the life of every literate person on the planet.

My examples gravitate towards medical doctors in this book for a reason. As a physician I am *in synch* with other physicians. It takes one to know one. Second, physicians, early on in their career already in medical school, realize that in order to find out their aspiration for a medical degree and obtain the licensure required to practice medicine they have to focus on their objectives without letting distractions stray them off course. On rare occasions a medical student manages to accomplish more than one major professional goal at the same time.

Years ago, during my subspecialty training, my mentor, Dr. Ann M. Lawrence, a physician of great academic achievements, mentioned to me that she did her research work in biochemistry while the other graduate student in the lab next door was Roger Bannister. He was running on a stationary bike while doing his work in the lab. Looking at my puzzled face, she went on to explain to me that this was the first man who ran a distance of one mile in less than four minutes. I made a mental note of her story but no more. It took me many years to appreciate the full implications of Roger Bannister's achievements. The point I am making is that every worthwhile endeavor of significance is carried out in alignment with the Key Concepts of the LOA. Read this chapter to the end to find the connection to Habakkuk.

∞⁀∾

Roger Bannister was born in 1929 in Harrow, England. He went to school in Oxford. At age seventeen he was attracted to competitive running. A year later in 1947 he ran a mile in 4 minutes and 24.6 seconds. In 1948 he watched the Olympic Games and was inspired by other athletes. So he set himself a goal to participate in the 1952 Olympic Games in Helsinki Finland.

Now get that. At that time the prevailing belief among the sports physiologists and sports pundits was that a man cannot run a mile in less than four minutes (240 seconds). The belief was that it is humanly impossible.

When everyone believes in something then this "something" must be the "truth." Cannot run a mile in less than four minutes? Then no one runs a mile in less than four minutes. You get no more than what you expect.

But a belief, any belief, is just a thought in a man's mind. A belief is not "the truth." Change your thought and you change your belief. Change your belief and you can manifest a different result.

Roger Bannister kept on training. In 1949 he ran a mile in 4 minutes and 14.2 seconds.

He kept training. In 1951 he ran a mile in 4 minutes and 7.8 seconds. The 1952 Olympic games came and went and Roger Bannister did not achieve his goal. He decided to re-commit himself to run a mile in less than four minutes.

In 1953 another great athlete ran a mile in 4 minutes and 3.6 seconds. Bannister wrote about it in his memoir: *"This race made me realize that the four minute mile was not out of reach."*

This thought was a pivotal change in Bannister's mindset. He realized that he could do it.

The LOA started to summon the thoughts and reinforce the belief that he will do it. He got his training organized methodically and prepared his body for the physical effort. In 1954 an Australian athlete, John Landy, ran a mile in 4 minutes and 2.4 seconds.

On May 6, 1954, in a track at Oxford University, Roger Bannister ran a mile in 3 minutes and 59.4 seconds. On August 7, 1954, Roger Bannister improved his personal record running one mile in 3 minutes and 58.8 seconds.

Roger Bannister debunked the common experts' tale that a mile cannot be run in less than 240 seconds. It is reported that a Frenchman asked of the first runner who ran a sub-four minute mile: "How did he know he would not die?"[87]

−⸱

Four lessons are embedded in the details of this story.

First—the old prevailing false belief that a mile cannot be run in less than four minutes. This belief was a myth propagated for many years by sports writers, and athletic pundits. It is thought that the main reason for the long life of this myth was caused by having to do with rounded numbers...

One mile. Four minutes. Rounded numbers.

There is nothing sacred in rounded numbers that governs human physiology. As a physiologist Roger Bannister knew that. He changed his beliefs. He subjected himself to a historic physiological experiment of great consequence.

---

87   Neal Bascomb: *The Perfect Mile.* Houghton Mifflin Company. Boston, New York. 2004. P. IX.

Second—Roger Bannister took his preparation training from the amateur level to the higher professional level. For that purpose he formed a *mastermind alliance* with a master trainer.

His trainer was *Franz Stampfl.*

To understand Roger Bannister we need to know who his mastermind ally was. The personal story of Franz Stampfl is in and by itself a tale of heroic personal achievement. Franz Stampfl was an athlete who earlier in his life had to perform against all odds under unusual physical circumstances in order to *survive* for his life. This heroic story is worth retelling and studying.

Franz Stampfl was a native of Austria who ran away from the Nazi regime in Austria looking for asylum in Britain. However, the British authorities deported Germans and Austrians to Canada and thence to Australia. The ship Stampfl was on board, SS Arandora Star, was attacked on July 2, 1940, by a German submarine and sank.

To survive Stampfl forced a side steel plate of the ship to break out from the ship to the surface and then jumped out into the freezing cold, oil-slicked waters of the North Sea. For eight hours he kept swimming and avoided freezing in the icy North Sea, until a rescue boat saved him. Eventually Stampfl returned to live in Britain in 1946.

For Franz Stampfl physical endurance was not a sport. It was a matter of life or death. There is every reason to believe that Stampfl shared and instilled this spirit of the *"will to win"* in Roger Bannister by his personal example.

Third—Roger Bannister demonstrated that a belief is only a thought. If you change your thought your belief is changed. When he changed his thought, his belief was changed and he busted the previous false belief.

Once he demonstrated that it is doable, other runners continued to improve on his record. Today the one mile running time record is 223.13 seconds.

The life story of Dr. Roger Bannister continued with success and distinction. As a person who found out what is required to align with the LOA, Dr. Bannister graduated from medical school and continued to conduct medical research in the area of the physiology of the autonomic nervous system. As a renowned athletic figure he was appointed in 1971 the first Chairmen of the British Sports Council. For his services to his country he was knighted. In 1984 Dr. Bannister was awarded an honorary doctoral degree.

Fourth—Dr. Bannister was a writer from early on in his career as an athlete and a medical student. He kept a diary and recorded his activities and training achievements. Bannister published in 1955 a memoir titled *The Four Minute Mile*. This book is still in demand 60 years later. In 2004 a new Fiftieth Anniversary Edition was published with a follow-up chapter and recent years' photographs.[88]

As you open Roger Bannister's memoir (1ˢᵗ edition) you read:

CHAPTER ONE
INTRODUCTION

Write the vision and make it plain upon tables, that he may run that readeth it.

Book of Habakkuk

The same text is in the Fiftieth-Anniversary Edition, Introduction chapter.

Serious athletes who want to excel in their area of sports and win an award will do themselves a great service by studying Dr. Bannister's memoir.

Ostensibly Dr. Bannister was aware of Habakkuk's proven prescription for manifesting successfully one's objectives and goals.

HabakkuK is forever, just like diamonds.

---

88   Roger Bannister: *The Four Minute Mile*. Fiftieth-Anniversary Edition. The Lyons Press. Guilford, Ct. 2004.

Chapter Fifteen

THE TOOL BOX
OF THE MASTER
ATTRACTORS

This chapter is your startup inventory list of the contents that are in the toolbox of triggers of LOA. This list of tools and ideas on how to activate the LOA is random and spontaneous. The LOA shrivels and wilts when presented with too rigid formatted instructions. The LOA blossoms and works best when allowed to produce extemporaneously and impulsively. Consider this chapter as a practical "how to." There is a known similarity among some items on the list and there is a degree of seeming repetitiveness.

Living in alignment with the Law of Attraction requires a mindset of instinctive and habitual familiarity with its Key Concepts and framework. With repeated practice the items on this list and many more will be your skill set—a life tool—for living in alignment with the Law of Attraction.

1. Job One
   Turn Your Thoughts Into Reality
   - You do it by writing your thoughts and visions on paper—you may also draw it or create an electronic file.

- Hand-writing and hand-drawing is the preferred method. It is more effective than recording first and transcribing later by another person. Using your motor neurons primes the brain towards manifesting the desired objective.
- Talk your thoughts aloud. Tell your ears and your listener what is your goal or destination.

Note: whatever you do—it is all about manifesting your objective, intention, goal, and destiny.

2. Write down your intentions, objectives or destination in life.
   - Get yourself a spiral notebook to write down your objectives. I find an unexplained magic in a spiral notebook more than a plain journal of ordinary binding. Use a pen to write. Journaling by using a word processor seems to me less effective than actual hand-writing.
   - Always date your entries.

3. Rewrite your goals and objectives and intentions from time to time.

4. Take photographs of your objective or destinations and paste it in your spiral notebook.
   - When feasible, include your own personal photographs pasted to your destination or goal entry.
   - When applicable add a map and relevant diagrams.

5. Paste photographs or diagrams of your desired goal or objective on your walls, doors or mirrors.
   - Create printed graphics of your goals, objectives or destination that are aesthetically appealing and attractive to your eyes and post them.
   - Continue to collect information about your goal or destination and save it in a scrap book or drop-file.

6. Go on internet Search Engines and extract information about your intentions, destination, goals, and objectives.

7. Go on YouTube and search, find and watch video footage about your goal and destination. Review this footage again periodically.

8. Go on Google Images and find photographs and diagrams of your destination, objective or desired intent. Save them. Print them. Paste them where you can review the photographs periodically.

- Soak in the graphic images with your eyes and mind.
9. Search for quotes about your object of interest. Go to a Search Engine, type and enter "Quotes on... [~ your search objective]."
10. Listen to inspirational music while you write in your spiral notebook.
11. Obtain journals, travel guides, maps and brochures of your destination or location, as the project may be, then read and soak in the information.
12. Write down a checklist of requirements to achieve your objective or destination.
    - Do not be concerned about the required resources at this stage or any future phase of manifestation. The universe is infinitely rich.
    - Put the LOA to test. Yes, let the LOA assemble the required matching components and resources for you.
    - Be prepared to study, do work, take an exam, or take a licensing test if required to reach your objective.
13. Take photographs of yourself next to, or in front of your desired objective.
    - You want a job in a store? Take a picture of you at the front or inside the store. Post your picture on your bedroom wall or mirror.
    - You want a position with an organization? Start your job search by taking a picture in front the organization's headquarters. Post it.
14. Shoot your own videos of your final destination or the accomplished goal. In the video show the desired ending as achieved or the destination when arrived at. It will manifest shortly thereafter.
15. Publish the contents you create.
    - Everyone is a publisher. Publishing includes all channels of distribution and broadcast.
16. Speak in public about your intention, goal or destination.
    - The act of public speaking integrates the neuronal brain circuits center responsible for speech and those recruit additional neuronal brain circuits towards attracting the necessary components required to manifest your thought into reality.

- Speak out and tell your intentions to yourself if necessary when no audience is available.
- Join a public speaking club. Take public speaking courses and develop your public speaking skills and confidence. In a short time you will be telling your thoughts in front of a live audience like a master attractor.

17. Form a mastermind alliance from among your friends, or join a mastermind alliance to advance the manifestation of your intent or objective.
    - Speak before your mastermind alliance.
    - Present a free seminar about your objective to your friends or a club.

18. Pray. Pray (ask) for the manifestation of your desired outcome.
    - Prayer reinforces the brain's neural circuits and embeds the desired outcome in the subconscious enhancing its manifestation.
    - All monotheistic religions have scheduled daily prayer 3 to 5 times every day.
    - Repeat your prayer mentally, verbally and in writing. Write down your prayer request. Many denominations take written prayer requests mailed in.

19. Create your own private rituals that connect you to your desired objective or goal. Some monotheistic religions have prayer beads while others have written prayer rituals such as phylacteries.

20. Imagery.
    - Imagine vividly in your mind's eye that which you want to create in your life. Repeat this mental exercise every day.

21. Manage your self-talk. Keep your self-talk positive, constructive and confident.
    - Use affirmative language. Use "can do" language.
    - Avoid conditional or doubtful words such as "but," "maybe" and "it depends."
    - If you express doubts the LOA will manifest your doubts.

22. Let your subconscious mind do the work of manifestation. Do not take conscious responsibility for the process of manifesting.

Let the new desired reality coalesce through aligning with the Law of Attraction.

23. Maintain a trusting disposition in the Law of Attraction to summon your required matching components of your desire. The LOA is always functioning in the background.

24. Assume the attitude of letting the LOA prove itself by delivering your objective to you. Put to test the validity and powers of the LOA.

25. The process of co-creation is always in alignment with the LOA and has no time boundaries.
    - *A desired goal or event has its own unique time-line to manifestation.*
    - The time-line of the universe is infinite. The universe has no deadline.

26. Always trust the LOA. Maintain a mindset of objective attitude by reminding yourself that the LOA bears its own proof.

27. Expect the delivery of your wish or goal via unforeseen, irregular, previously unfamiliar channels of supply sources.
    - Live a life of *benestrophic* expectations.

28. Expect and accept unusual and irregular contributions towards manifesting your creation through unforeseen channels. Positive expectation clears the road to serendipitous occurrences. For example:
    - Expect to win money, receive grants and bonuses.
    - Expect contributions from strangers.

29. Look forwards meeting new friends, partners and allies who will support you.

30. Strike mutually beneficial agreements with other people.

31. Be generous to others. Pay it forward—cast your bread over the water.

32. Bless other people. Always forgive and avoid grudges.

33. Enjoy the beauty of nature. Every season is uniquely beautiful.

34. Show reverence for life. Respect all forms of life.

35. Mental activity precedes every act of manifestation.

36. Every human being—manifests.
    - Co-create alone or with your friends.

37. Think at all times about your desired future as you want to see it manifested.

- The present is already a manifestation of your past thinking. Do not dwell on the past because it will manifest again in your future.
- Use the present moment for constructive and positive awareness.

38. Sense now the emotional feelings of your end-game manifestation.

39. Follow your passion. Following your passion is the right decision for you. Another decision will be a dead-end.

40. Meditate regularly.
    - Take time to stay in a state of stillness. Mind chatter interferes with attainment of higher wisdom and enlightenment.

41. Hang out with friends who aligned their life with the Law of Attraction.

42. Believe in your goal and objectives.
    - Belief provides the energy to manifest your vision.
    - Belief stabilizes the right mindset for creativity and manifestation.

43. Take a break from intending, wishing, and goal setting. Once you formulated your desire, sit still for a while and do no more about it.
    - Test the Law of Attraction by letting the universe deliver your wish to you.
    - Just watch for the delivery of your desired objective.

44. Keep the neuronal circuits of your brain agile, alert, and reflexive.
    - Perform daily mental exercises: solve puzzles, do Sudoku riddles.
    - Think differently!

45. Periodically re-focus your thoughts on what you do want.

46. What you now want represents your future. Then cooperative components are assembled to manifest your projected future.

47. Expect and watch for *serendipitous* events conducive to the manifestation of your objective or goal.

48. Expect and recognize synchronous mental occurrences at all time. *Synchronicity* occurs both during conscious and wakeful time and during sleep time. The reticular activating system and the default neuronal network in our brain are always operating.

49. Pray. Prayer is a form of asking. Prayer activates the LOA framework.

50. If you are in need of a cure and restoration of health, start by looking for a healer or medical doctor with a "can do, can treat, can cure" attitude.

    • Stay away from a physician who tells you that you have only so many months remaining to live, or that the prognosis is "guarded" (euphemism to "bad prognosis"), will not cure you or your loved one. Their negative attitude attracts disease and agony.

51. Draw a grid-like diagram and let it represent your goal or destination. In every cell enter a word, term or number that you think is related to your objective.

    • Make it an Excel-like spreadsheet if you wish to use software.

52. Draw a mind-map starting with your objective in the center. Branch out off shoots and leaves with details of your desired objective.

    • Study how to make mind-maps. Mind-maps will activate your creative mind.

    • Go to Google Images and search for "project management methodologies." Enrich your mind with the colorful alternatives.

53. Add here triggers of your own that activate the Law of Attraction for you.

    • Add at least ten more triggers of your own.

    • Share your triggers on this book affiliated blog: www.themasterattractor.blogspot.com

Conclusion

WHAT IT ALL
MEANS FOR YOU

I n conclusion, what is in it for you?

Since you acquired this book and read it thus far, you are a person who has an idea as to what you want. If you did not have a clue what you want you would not buy this book nor read it. I assume fairly so that you are looking for results in your life. You want to manifest some things.

You want to turn your thoughts into reality.

The LOA reassures you that you can attract and manifest. This book outlines to you how to get your life in alignment with the LOA. The Bible has documented proven methods to get you where you want to be. The methods are tried and tested throughout history.

You do not need to be a person of a certain denomination in order to manifest following the methods told in the Bible. You do not need to be a Christian or Jew. The LOA works in support of any person who lives in alignment with its Key Concepts and framework. The LOA supports you in becoming who you want to be.

The most celebrated modern evangelists lived and carried their missions in alignment with the LOA.

✧✦✧

Titans of business and industry worked in alignment with the LOA. Paul Arden (1940–2008) was Executive Creative Director at the advertising agency, Saatchi & Saatchi. Arden was regarded as a creative genius. He was responsible for attracting millions of buyers to the firm's clients. Arden knew how to attract people. In his book titled *It's Not How Good You Are, It's how Good you want To Be*, he wrote:

> *Your vision of where or who you want to be is the greatest asset you have.*
> *Without having a goal it's difficult to score.*

The Law of Attraction was known to the authors and editors of the Bible. Humankind knew the essential elements that pertain to the function of the LOA at the time when the Bible was written and canonized. The Bible offers counsel and suggestions on how to live life in alignment with LOA. It warns people who disregard the subtleties of the rules of the LOA—Know where you want to go.

✧✦✧

Steve Jobs (1955–2011) revolutionized the information and communication technologies with his four innovations—first with the Mac computer and then with the *i*Pod, *i*Pad and *i*Phone. We no longer imagine civilized life without these inventions or their compatible equipment. He wrote:

> *Life can be much broader once you discover one simple fact: Everything around you that you call life was made up by people that were no smarter than you and you can change it, you can influence it. You can build your own things that other people can use. Once you learn that, you'll never be the same again.*

∽⊱⊰∾

Tim Tebow, the American football player, is a nascent master attractor.[89] Tebow is credited with several achievements in Pro Football. His style of praying while bowing in public before the game gave birth to the term "Tebowing." It is very likely that consistent praying before every game helped him focus on his performance on the field and achieving the success for which he is now famed.

∽⊱⊰∾

If you are still not sure where you want to go or do then get up and take a walk anywhere. Turn off your TV. Go to the park, go to the mall, go to the movies, go to school. Wherever you go, you will meet new people. Chances are that other people will inspire an attractive idea where to turn further or what next to do.

Just show up among the people. Follow Woody Allen's advice:

Eighty percent of success is showing up.

∽⊱⊰∾

Every pilot is required prior to takeoff to submit a flight plan with the local air traffic control tower. Commercial pilots refer to it as "completing the paperwork" prior to getting permission for takeoff. The captain and the first officer may then say a safe trip prayer.

The flight course is subject to midflight corrections. That is obvious. The winds change direction and speed; a passenger may develop an emergency. Nonetheless, the aircraft with rare exceptions lands at its destination.

You are the Captain of your life. Do you have a written flight plan for your life?

---

89   His personal Facebook page showed over 1.2 million subscribers by end of 2011. The page is now gone. (http://themasterattractor.blogspot.com/2011/12/tim-tebow-nascent-master-attractor.html).

APPENDIX I

TEN KEY CONCEPTS OF THE LAW OF ATTRACTION

Thinking people co-create their reality.

Every person must have a unique vision for their life.

Write down your vision and goals.

The LOA provides limitless channels for manifestation.

Begin where you are by acting in alignment with your vision.

Engage and utilize a mastermind alliance.

The LOA manifests through infinite springs of abundance.

The LOA operates by inclusion. It does not discriminate.

Hold on to your faith. The Just lives by his faith.

The LOA is a gift that keeps on giving.

Appendix II

I like to see and witness things for myself. If I was not present there when it happened the least I can do is go see where it happened. As I wrote this book I went to visit two sites where, according to local tradition and the New Testament, Jesus manifested abundance and healing.

VISITING TABGHA

Tabgha is located about a mile south of Capernaum on the northwest shore of the Lake of Galilee. During the first four centuries CE, a Christian community of Jewish descent lived in Capernaum. It is possible that this community preserved the memory and passed the stories about Jesus down the generations. A pilgrim, Lady Egeria, visited Tabgha circa 383 CE. Close to the seven springs (*Heptapegon* in Greek) there were some rock formations and one rock was said to mark the place were Jesus fed the multitudes with five loaves and two fish. The first church was built around the rock by Yosipos of Tiberias circa 350 CE. The structure was enlarged in 450 CE into a Byzantine style church. It is thought that the rock was moved slightly and placed in position under the altar. The floor was decorated with beautiful mosaics. Among the visitors to Tabgha were St. Paula and St. Jerome. The church was destroyed in 614 CE by the Persians. In 670 CE, Bishop Arculf visited the place and saw columns lying around the fountains' edge.

The ruins of Tabgha remained abandoned for 1,300 years, and rediscovered in 1932 by German archeologists who found the mosaics. A new church was built over the ruins of the ancient church. The church has simple architecture and draws its exquisiteness from the ancient beautiful mosaics that were preserved and the mystic aura of the legend—The Church of Multiplication (of the loaves and fish).

Many large eucalyptus and palm trees surround the monastery and provide refreshing shade in the heat of the valley of Genussar (Genussareth). In the courtyard of the monastery is a plaque explaining the significance of the place with quotes from the New Testament. There is a youth hostel on-site and a concession shop for literature, souvenirs and refreshments (cold water is the best). The property belongs to the German Association of the Holy Land run by the Archbishop of Cologne, Germany. The Benedictine priors of the Dormition manage the place.

For more information visit: www.tabgha.net (text in German).

The interior of the Church of Multiplication in Tabgha (Heptapegon).

Under the altar is the rock where it is said that Jesus blessed on the loaves and fish.

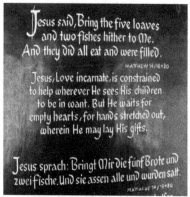

The mosaic of loaves and fish.

Quote from Matthew 14:18, posted on the church wall.

Visiting Nain

Nain (or Nein) is a small Arab village on the north slope of the Hill of Moreh, a few miles from Mount Tabor and nine miles southeast of Nazareth. Unlike Tabgha there are no permanent records of physical ruins or remains, which make a landmark in that area to represent an obvious site of event where Jesus resurrected the boy (as described in Luke 7:11–17). In the 19th century the Biblical scholars Edward Robinson and Eli Smith visited the site and identified Nain as the location mentioned by Luke. They likely received this information from the local Muslim residents.

Nain was mentioned by Eusebius and by Jerome in the 4th century as being located near the village of Eindor. The legend has it that the Crusaders recognized the site and built there a commemorative church. However, today there are no ruins or remains of older or ancient church structures. The Franciscan order built in Nain a small church, very simple in its architecture. The custodian of the church is an Arab-Muslim family and there were no Christians in sight during my two visits.

Inside the church is a plaque in Italian and Latin that commemorates the significance of the place. There are two oil-on-canvas paintings in the church, one above the entrance door and another above the altar.

You may visit the chapel any day. When you show up, a family member living in a house next to the chapel will come out and open the door for you to enter and visit.

Exterior and entrance to
the church in Nain.

Simple interior of
the church in Nain.

Jesus cures the boy. Painting
above the entrance door.

Jesus delivers the boy to mother.
Painting above the altar.

SOURCES

The author consulted, compared, or quoted in the course of writing the following Bible editions:

Single folio of the KJV. London. Robert Barker. 1611.

Facsimile of KJV. 1611. Quad-centennial Subscribers' Edition. 2009. Published by the Bible Museum. Goodyear, Arizona.

Holy Bible KJV. Thomas Nelson Bibles. 1994. 2003. 2005.

The New Oxford Bible. Annotated Bible with the Apocrypha. Oxford University Press. USA. 2007.

The Aleppo Codex. A facsimile edition. (Hebrew) Magnes Publishing House. Jerusalem Israel.

The Leningrad Codex. A Facsimile Edition. Wm B. Eerdmans Publishing Co. Grand Rapids, Michigan. 1998. (Hebrew and English introduction).

The Parallel Bible Hebrew-English Old Testament. With the Biblia Hebraica Leningradensia, and the King James Version. Hendrickson Publishers, Inc. Peabody, Massachusetts. 2003.

Biblia Hebraica Shtuttgartensia.

Online versions of the Septuagint (http://spindleworks.com/septuagint); and the Vulgate (http://www.perseus.tufts.edu).

The TANACH. (Hebrew). Koren Publishing. Jerusalem, Israel. 2005.

The New Testament (Hebrew). Translated from Greek (Elzevir edition). Leyden (1624), into Hebrew by Franz Delitzsch, (1877). Lowe and Brydone Printers. London 1948.

Scholarly volumes consulted for historical and factual research include:

John MacArthur: "The MacArthur Bible Commentary" Thomas Nelson Inc. Nashville TN. 2005.

All other quotes were referenced in footnotes in the text.

STUDY GUIDE

Chapter One

- Is the LOA a psychological or a metaphysical phenomenon?
- Where in the Bible is the closest description of the LOA? Book____ Chapter____ Verse____
- List the "tools" the author cites that enable the LOA.
- What is a mastermind alliance?
- Does the LOA work for select persons or for all humanity?
- List three great biblical manifesters.
- What happens in the absence of a vision? Book____ Chapter____ Verse____

Chapter Five

- What is required for attracting health and wellness?
- Why do spiritual leaders and prophets get sick and die like all humans?
- How can you attract health and wellness?

Chapter Six

- What are the four tools the prophet Habakkuk uses to ensure the LOA will bring about the desired manifestation?
- Why Habakkuk is repeatedly cited in the New Testament and later theologians?

Chapter Fourteen

- Who is the athlete holding first-ever world record who cites Habakkuk?

The Key Concepts of LOA

- Which Key Concept is most fundamental for the LOA?

Note: some discussion questions have more than one answer.

ACKNOWLEDGEMENTS

I am indebted to the many masters of the Law of Attraction from whom I learned all I know. I heard about the Law of Attraction from Napoleon Hill, Earl Nightingale, and Denis Waitley, early on. Mark Victor Hansen, a master attractor, directed my attention to the prophet HabakkuK—the biblical master attractor. Bruce Wilkinson introduced me to Jabez whom God gave all that he asked. I still continue to gain deep insights from the live seminars and videos of Esther Hicks (and her friends Abraham), the prophetess of LOA. The author Joe Vitale has practical ideas on how to benefit from the LOA. There are numerous other authors that enlarged my vistas of the LOA. Thank you all.

The publishers at the former Intermedia Publishing group, Terry Whalin and Larry Davis encouraged me with advice. At the home front, Charles Roger Gillen III, and Travis Tenwalde, (old friends of HabakkuK) extended their support in getting the work done and getting the word out. They still do.

Prof. Minna Rozen of Haifa University is always my source of inspiration and omniscient counsel on all Judeo-Christian questions that I have. Her knowledge in the ancient Mediterranean languages of Latin, Greek, Turkish, Aramaic and Hebrew is incredible. She quotes Jabez and HabakkuK right from the Greek Septuagint. She knows more than one secret. Thank you Minna.

I am grateful to Ms. Lori Morningstar Villarreal for editing and formatting this manuscript.

ABOUT THE AUTHOR

Mandy (Menahem) Lender lives in the U.S. Born in Israel, he graduated from the Hebrew University in Jerusalem, Israel, and the Dominican University, River Forest, Illinois. Dr. Lender volunteers as a physician helping patients lacking health insurance at the Helen M. Nickless free clinic in Bay City, Michigan. Dr. Lender is a battlefield combat survivor and a cancer survivor. He completed a memoir based on his experience as a cancer patient—*Karkinos Farm*. (www.karkinosfarm.com). As a public speaker, Dr. Lender is available to share his knowledge on the Law of Attraction (particularly attracting health), and its biblical corollaries. Write him by e-mail: mandy@mandy1st.com with any question.

Join '*Mandy Lender*' as his friend on Facebook and Google+. If you read this book, so far you are a confirmed friend!

Dr. Lender web-site:

www.mandylender.com

Blogs by Dr. Lender:

www.mandylender.wordpress.com

www.themasterattractor.blogspot.com

www.inspiredbyhabakkuk.blogspot.com

www.fourstatesbooksigning.blogspot.com

INDEX